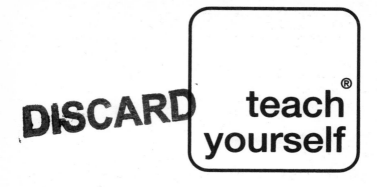

DISCARD

teach yourself ®

**saving energy
in the home**

**saving energy
in the home**
nick white

Launched in 1938, the **teach yourself** series
grew rapidly in response to the world's wartime
needs. Loved and trusted by over 50 million
readers, the series has continued to respond to
society's changing interests and passions and
now, 70 years on, includes over 500 titles,
from Arabic and Beekeeping to Yoga and Zulu.
What would you like to learn?

be where you want to be with **teach yourself**

Disclaimer

The costs and payback calculations shown in the book are approximate, and provided for illustrative purposes only – we accept no liability whatsoever for the accuracy or reliability of the calculations. Ensure you check current prices.

Orders: please contact Bookpoint Ltd, 130 Milton Park, Abingdon, Oxon OX14 4SB. Telephone: +44 (0) 1235 827720. Fax: +44 (0) 1235 400454. Lines are open 09.00–17.00, Monday to Saturday, with a 24-hour message answering service. You can also order through our website www.hoddereducation.co.uk

British Library Cataloguing in Publication Data: a catalogue record for this title is available from the British Library.

Library of Congress Catalog Card Number: on file.

First published in UK 2008 by Hodder Education, part of Hachette Livre UK, 338 Euston Road, London, NW1 3BH.

This edition published 2008.

The **teach yourself** name is a registered trade mark of Hodder Headline.

Typeset by Transet Limited, Coventry, England.
Printed in Great Britain for Hodder Education, an Hachette Livre UK Company, 338 Euston Road, London NW1 3BH, by Cox & Wyman Ltd, Reading, Berkshire.

The publisher has used its best endeavours to ensure that the URLs for external websites referred to in this book are correct and active at the time of going to press. However, the publisher and the author have no responsibility for the websites and can make no guarantee that a site will remain live or that the content will remain relevant, decent or appropriate.

Hachette Livre UK's policy is to use papers that are natural, renewable and recyclable products and made from wood grown in sustainable forests. The logging and manufacturing processes are expected to conform to the environmental regulations of the country of origin.

Impression number   10 9 8 7 6 5 4 3 2 1
Year   2012 2011 2010 2009 2008

R0429857753

v

contents

acknowledgements

I would first like to acknowledge the wealth of knowledge and experience gained over ten years from being part of the Hockerton Housing Project; living in the ultra low energy homes, installing renewable energy systems, being part of an eco-community and developing an eco-business supporting others to achieve greater levels of sustainability.

More personally I would like to thank all of the members of the Hockerton Housing Project (Simon, Helena, Trudi, Pete, Nick, Sandy, Bill and Louise) for supporting me in writing the book, and in particular Simon for acting as my technical sanity check, and Bill for drawing some of the images.

During my many months of researching for the book, the richest vein of information came from the Energy Saving Trust (EST) who through their website and advice centres, do a fantastic job. I would like to particularly thank Emily Batchelor and other members of the EST Data Services team, who laboriously checked over many of my figures. There were, however, many other sources of information, too numerous to mention, collected over a long period of time and itching to be put into print.

Finally I want to reserve my main gratitude, thanks and love to my darling wife, Trudi, who has not only had to share my frustrations and long hours at the computer, but very generously acted as chief sub-editor – fine-tuning, correcting, providing guidance and encouragement. Oh, and of course my kids (Rebecca, Francesca, and Freya) who have seen far too little of their father over the summer of 2007.

preface

Little did I know the task ahead when I was contacted by Hodder to write this book. I had for many years thought about writing a straightforward practical book about energy saving in the home. This started, I suppose, because of an old gardener's cottage that I lived in with my family in the early 90s. Energy prices were not anywhere near as high in real terms as they are now, but being an old detached cottage with all four single brick walls braced against the wind, it leaked heat like a sieve. The result was damp walls and ridiculous bills. I could never work out how the central heating system worked as the previous owner was a DIY enthusiast! There seemed to be no easy way to find out what to do about improving the situation. Hence my idea of researching and writing a book.

But then in 1996 my family had the opportunity of joining an eco-community self-build project in Nottinghamshire: the Hockerton Housing Project. Within months we had sold up, moved into a caravan, and started to build our own zero-heated, ultra low energy homes with four other families. Ten years on, our earth-sheltered home has used less than £5 on space heating, whilst never going below 18 °C. Overall we only use ten per cent of the energy we used in our previous cottage, and most of that we meet with wind and solar power. But this is another story and another book.

I feel very grateful to have had the opportunity of joining the Hockerton Housing Project and going on a very real and practical journey of creating the ultimate in low energy living. I hope experiences of living in very different types of properties have allowed me to reflect in this book, realism but also aspiration, both in financial and environmental terms. By the way my last quarterly energy bill was £15.70!

It was interesting and challenging, therefore, writing a book about 'normal' houses. I had to think back to my days in the cottage and not get too carried away with zero-heating and community wind turbines. What I did discover was how many simple things people could do to make a big difference to their energy use, many just behavioural. I wish you all the best in saving money and doing your bit for the planet.

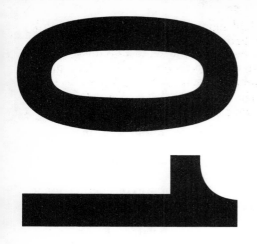

01

background to energy use

In this chapter you will learn:
- the importance of saving energy to reduce household costs and environmental impact
- how improving the energy efficiency of your home can increase its marketability
- what the energy currencies are
- about carbon.

Why save energy?

You may find at least part of the answer to this question by asking yourself why you picked up this book in the first place and started to flick through its pages.

- Perhaps you've recently received a higher than expected energy bill and you want to reduce your future energy costs.
- Maybe you've become concerned about the increasing number of news stories on the TV, radio or in the papers about climate change caused by the burning of fossil fuels to provide energy.
- You may have recently moved house or are considering doing so, and you are concerned about the energy efficiency of the property, particularly with the recent introduction of 'Home Information Packs' and the associated Environment Performance Certificate.
- Or it may actually be a combination or all the above factors.

Whatever the reason, it makes a lot of sense to reduce energy use, and no sense at all to keep wasting it. The burning of fossil fuels to provide heat, light and run the electrical appliances in our homes accounts for over a quarter of the UK's carbon dioxide (CO_2) emissions. We produce a similar amount of CO_2 emissions by burning petrol and diesel to run our cars, and we purchase products and materials whose manufacture requires energy, and furthermore, in doing so we cause greenhouse gas emissions. We have potentially great influence over reducing these emissions. There are many different ways to save energy, starting from no cost or inexpensive means involving anything from small changes in habits, to large investment choices such as installing microgeneration systems on our homes. Many options will be explored in Chapters 04–07. In the meantime, this chapter will provide more information about the benefits of saving energy for you and the environment.

American note!

While the sources of information for this book, including energy standards and legislation, are largely UK based, the principles and much of the practical advice is applicable to any modern home, wherever in the world. For many of the relevant products there is an increasingly global 'look' to efficiency standards, which should mean that those referenced in this book are not too unfamiliar.

There will be some variation depending on local climate, building styles, product availability and use of technologies. For instance, US homes tend to be larger with a higher dependency on technologies, such as air-con units to control internal temperatures. This may affect the focus for energy-saving actions.

Finally, costs are all based on UK prices – to calculate local costs you will have to consider current exchange rates, your energy prices and local material costs to assess more accurately the impact on savings.

Reduce your energy costs

There has perhaps never been a better time to consider reducing your energy bills. From 2003 to 2007 gas bills rose by 71 per cent and electricity bills by 45 per cent! (Source: Ofgem). This means that the average household's total energy bill is over £1,000 for the first time. Also, since most of us pay our energy bills out of taxed income, you may actually need to earn nearer £1,500 to cover your energy costs. The good news is that it is relatively easy to reduce this amount through simple energy-savings measures.

A typical three-bedroom semi-detached house without any insulation might save several hundred pounds a year on heating costs through implementing some simple measures.

Are my energy bills likely to go up in the future?

The recent sharp increase in domestic energy costs has mainly been due to the rising costs of fossil fuels (oil, coal and gas) and the growing demand to cut polluting carbon emissions. The UK is increasingly reliant on European gas imports as its own reserves have declined; prices for European gas are more volatile as they reflect relative changes in oil price.

Wholesale prices for gas and other fuels may fall in the short term as new competition enters the UK energy market and new import sources, mainly from Europe, become more reliable and bulk prices stabilize. However, it is likely that in the medium to long term energy prices will rise further for a number of reasons:

- Increasing global demand for diminishing energy supplies.
- Greater uncertainty about the future supply and reliability of oil and gas as the UK moves from being an energy exporter to an energy importer.
- Volatility of supply and prices of oil.
- Increasing financial investment by energy suppliers in alternative, renewable energy supplies. Currently every householder pays an additional £7 per annum in the energy bill to support this investment. This is predicted to increase to £20 by 2015.
- Increasing financial investment by energy suppliers in energy efficiency – currently this adds £9 per customer per fuel each year.

In conclusion, any energy-saving measures you make now are likely to help you protect your household from significant future increases in energy costs.

Does it pay to invest in energy saving?

There are a wide range of options to reduce energy use from 'no cost' simple lifestyle changes to more serious financial investments such as installing renewable energy systems in your home. Clearly, zero to low cost options makes financial sense and their implementation is more about awareness and motivation of house occupants.

Consumers want financial incentives to go green

Half of all British consumers think it would be too expensive to make their homes energy efficient, but a growing number say they would go green if they were offered financial incentives. According to a new survey from home insurer MORE TH>N, eight out of ten would consider making environmental improvements to their homes if they could get a reduction in their council tax; 29 per cent would be swayed by lower mortgage rates, and six out of ten would make an effort if there was evidence that it would make their homes significantly cheaper to run. (Source: Green Building Magazine website – **www.newbuilder.co.uk**)

As with any financial investment, the decision to spend a significant sum of money on an energy-saving feature (such as installing solar panels) needs to involve an assessment of the rate of return on that investment. A payback calculation of how many years it will it take to recoup the initial capital cost through the energy savings you will make is simple to do:

$$\text{Payback (number of years)} = \frac{\text{Capital cost (£)}}{\text{Annual energy savings (£)}}$$

This means that higher energy prices or reduced installation costs (e.g. through obtaining a grant) will decrease the payback period, making any investment more worthwhile.

For many of the investment actions suggested in this book, guidance is provided on likely costs, energy savings and payback. This will help you decide on the level of investment you are comfortable with at any one point in your energy-saving programme.

Homeowners are green, but only to save money, not the planet

UK homeowners think about green issues as long as it saves them money and doesn't inconvenience them, a survey finds. The PrimeMove.com survey revealed that 94 per cent of those polled considered energy efficiency important in their homes. However, 65 per cent of these revealed that their main motivator for adopting energy efficient measures was only to save money, with saving the planet and lowering carbon emissions coming second and third.

Insulation, double glazing and energy efficient light bulbs were the most popular measures homeowners were most likely to adopt or had adopted to help make their homes more energy efficient. Rainwater harvesting, wind turbines and solar panels were the least likely green initiatives to be installed. (Source: **PrimeMove.com**.)

Reduce your environmental impact

Every time you drive your car, switch on a light, turn on the central heating, or simply open a fridge door, you use energy. Whether we burn fuel directly as with gas or petrol, or indirectly as with electricity generated from fossil fuels, the energy produced will result in the release of carbon dioxide (CO_2) into the atmosphere. CO_2 is one of the main gases contributing to global warming. Hardly a week goes by now without another press headline or news bulletin warning us of the dangers we face from climate change.

Climate change

What is it?

The burning of fossil fuels for power and transport leads to emissions of greenhouse gases such as CO_2. These gases, that also occur naturally, trap some of the sun's energy which results in a warming of the earth's surface. Most scientists now agree that human activities have artificially accelerated this process.

figure 1.1 greenhouse effect

What are the likely affects?

Climate change is the most serious environmental threat to the planet. It is causing many areas of the world to experience an increase in extreme weather such as floods, storms, heat waves and droughts. It is leading to rising sea levels which is increasing the risk of coastal flooding in low-lying areas. Wildlife is being severely affected and diseases, such as malaria, are spreading as global temperatures rise.

Scientists predict that average global temperatures are set to rise by between two and six degrees Celsius this century. The ten hottest years since records began in 1850 have all been since 1990, with 1998 being the hottest year and 2005 the second hottest. (Source: Hadley Centre, Met Office.)

Some of the changes are potentially beneficial, but most impacts are likely to be negative, costly and disruptive. Behind the stories, real people are severely affected, with climate change now killing hundreds of thousands of people every year.

So far, although the UK has not experienced such extreme climate change as some parts of the world, it has already felt the impact with warmer summers and milder winters. The 2003 heatwave killed more than 30,000 people across Europe, including over 2,000 people in Britain. It was the biggest natural disaster in Europe on record, according to the UK Government's chief scientific adviser, Sir David King. (Source: Guardian Unlimited, 26 July, 2006.)

Nearly five million people in England and Wales live in flood risk zones and could be affected by rising water levels. There will also be an impact on our wildlife and plants, particularly those that cannot adapt so quickly or move.

> Britain's barnacles, limpets and seaweeds are moving north and east in response to climate change. (Source: BBC website, Dec 06.)

Elsewhere in Europe the impact will be more severe, in particular Spain, whose beaches are predicted to be too inhospitable due to excessive heat by the end of the century.

Other environmental problems

There are other environmental effects of our energy use:

- Depletion of non-renewable resources – oil has many other valuable uses other than burning for energy, for example, as a raw material in the manufacture of plastics.
- Toxic pollution such as oil spills.
- Acid rain – sulphur dioxide from power plants mixes with rain to produce a weak acid which affects wildlife, trees and insects.

What contribution am I making?

The public has an important role to play in tackling climate change, since the energy we use in our homes and for our personal transport accounts for 44 per cent of the UK's CO_2 emissions – and it's increasing. According to the 2007 report 'Positive Energy', by the Institute of Public Policy Research (IPPR), between 1990 and 2005, energy use in the home rose by 40 per cent and by nearly 23 per cent in the transport sector.

However, although most of us accept that climate change is happening and see it as the result of human action (and many of us are also worried about the implications), the evidence is that we are doing fairly little to reduce our emissions. The reasons for this are thought to be:

- a lack of awareness of how we contribute to the problem
- a lack of awareness of how we can most effectively and practically make a difference
- a sense that our contribution is so small that it is unlikely to make any difference
- a belief that it is not our responsibility to take action to reduce emissions, but the responsibility of the Government, industry or other countries
- a lack of financial incentives to change behaviour or invest in energy efficiency
- a desire for greater comfort and entertainment.

See Appendix 1 (What's stopping you save energy?) to assess your readiness for action.

According to IPPR's 2007 report, 'Positive Energy', millions of homes in the UK are still not properly insulated and have inefficient boilers that need replacing. Although we are increasingly buying energy-efficient A-rated appliances, the energy savings from these have been more than offset by the fact that we own a greater number of electrical goods, especially consumer electronics. Exacerbating the problem further, some new products consume more electricity than the products they replace; for example, plasma televisions consume four and a half times more energy than their cathode ray tube predecessors.

By contrast, only 0.4 per cent of households have installed renewable energy systems in their homes and only 0.83 per cent of homes have switched to 'green' tariff electricity (electricity that energy companies have produced from renewable sources of energy).

A similar picture exists for our transport choices, according to the IPPR report. We are using our cars to travel further and more often. There were 7.5 million more cars on the road in 2005 compared to 1990. Although there has been an increase in public transport use, it still makes up only eight per cent of the total number of trips made. Only London has seen a shift away from car use to buses and an increase in cycling. Outside of the capital, local bus use has declined and cycling represents only 1.5 per cent of all journeys made. Technological advances have reduced emissions from cars but few motorists recognize the concept of energy-efficient driving.

> Many of our small everyday actions have an impact. Simply 'Googling' or downloading from 'U-Tube' causes a series of servers to whir into action and burn up a bit more energy.

Although it's quite difficult to get an accurate assessment of exactly how much CO_2 each individual is responsible for, a recent study by the Carbon Trust (a Government-funded body) has tried to provide a more accurate assessment. They concluded that the average Briton is responsible for about 11 tonnes of CO_2, roughly half that of an American, but considerably more than people from developing nations. As a nation, the UK contributes about two per cent of global man-made emissions of CO_2. This may seem rather small, particularly when you then go down to an individual level. However, it is only by every individual taking personal responsibility and then taking action, accumulated across a population and then worldwide, that we can hope to avert serious environmental catastrophes.

> 'We will not solve this problem if we do not each take our share of the responsibility for tackling it. Nobody can protect themselves from climate change unless we protect each other by building a global basis for climate security. To put it starkly, if we all try to free ride, we will all end up in free fall, with accelerating climate change the result of our collective failure to respond in time to this shared threat.' (Margaret Becket, Secretary of State for Foreign and Commonwealth Affairs, United Kingdom of Great Britain and Northern Ireland, 5 June 2007, World Environment Day, UNEP)

figure 1.2 was it worth it? (Source: Polyp)

Increase the marketability of your home

Until recently most people paid little attention to the energy efficiency of a property when they were considering buying or selling. However, with the growing public awareness of the financial and environmental costs of energy use, an energy-efficient house will be potentially more attractive to purchasers. In addition, there is an increasing amount of legislation, including Building Regulations, which emphazise the energy efficiency of properties and applies to home-sellers, self-builders, renovators and leaseholders.

The recent introduction of 'Home Information Packs', which includes the requirement for an Environmental Performance Certificate (EPC) (see Chapter 02) will increase consumer awareness of the energy use of their home and the possible implications this may have on their property's value and saleability. For the first time, homebuyers will have access to a clear assessment of the relative energy use of one property versus another, which may well affect the house they choose to buy and how much they are willing to pay for it! There may be still further incentives created by EPCs – in England, sixteen councils have already piloted schemes with energy companies where council tax rebates are offered to people who make energy-saving changes to their homes, based on information from EPCs.

Simple changes you make to improve the energy efficiency of your home will be more cost effective in attracting buyers than showing off the latest fancy green gadget. Being able to demonstrate how well your home performs through energy bills and an EPC will be a powerful marketing tool when you come to sell your home.

Furthermore, consumer interest in the energy efficiency of properties is likely to increase in the future. Research has shown that younger people are generally more aware of green issues and attach greater value to them. It is these people who will increasingly become the future house-purchasers and they may be far more demanding of greater environmental standards than the current market.

Hidden values!

Consumer research commissioned by the Energy Saving Trust (EST) in January 2006 showed that buyers are willing to pay up to £10,000 more for an environmentally-friendly home. The same research also shows that although buyers may be initially swayed by a lick of paint or a mowed lawn, more than two thirds look past cosmetic improvements to more important factors, such as the condition of the boiler or the quality of the windows.

Green homes have more appeal for buyers

According to a 2007 study by Nationwide Building Society, the majority of UK homebuyers preferred a house with environmentally-friendly features. Given the choice between two properties of a similar size and value, 82 per cent of respondents claimed a house with features such as solar panels had more of an influence on their decision to buy than attic rooms (68 per cent), period features (63 per cent) and walk-in wardrobes (62 per cent).

(Research based on a sample of 1,000 respondents, conducted by Marketing Sciences' Panelwizard for Nationwide Building Society, March 2007.)

Common energy currency for the home

Throughout this book and more generally you will hear references to watts, kilowatts, kilowatt-hours (kWh), $kgCO_2$ and tonnes of CO_2. These are the terms of common currency that are used to measure and compare the financial and environmental costs of energy use. Currently householders are simply charged by fuel type (e.g. electricity, gas and oil) in kWh units to supply energy for their homes. However, increasingly we will be charged additional costs for the associated CO_2 emissions to try and reduce our environmental impact.

What is a watt?

The watt (symbol: W) is a unit of power. For example, a typical household light bulb uses electrical energy at a rate of 40 to 100 watts, and a low energy version at 9 to 15 watts. A kilowatt (symbol: kW) is equal to 1,000 watts.

Financial currency

However, to calculate the cost of power we need to multiply the power rating of the system or appliance being used, by the time it is operated. This is most commonly measured as kilowatt-hour (kWh), which is how you will see it referred to on your energy bill.

Power rating (in W or kW) × time in operation (hours) = kWh

For example:

- 100W light bulb (0.1kW) left on for 10 hours = (0.1kW × 10h) = 1kWh
- 10W low energy light bulb (0.01kW) left on for 10 hours = (0.01kW × 10h) = 0.1kWh
- Hair dryer (1kW) used for 1 hour = (1kW × 1h) = 1kWh
- Microwave (750W) used for 45 minutes = (0.75kW × 0.75h) = 0.56kWh
- 3kW immersion left on for 1 hour = (3kW × 1h) = 3kWh

You will then be charged based on the number of kilowatt-hours (kWh) consumed over the billing period. From the examples above you can see that it can be difficult to predict the actual cost of running different appliances. Some very power-hungry equipment is only used for very short periods of time and so may not use as much energy as others with lower ratings that are left running for much longer. This is further complicated as most homes use a mixture of fuels, for example, gas and electricity, that have different costs. Currently, the average costs are about 10p per/kWh for electricity and 2.5p per/kWh for gas. The cost of a specific fuel can vary during the day, often being cheaper during low demand periods (off-peak), for example, at night. Table 1.1 provides an indication of the current range in prices for different fuels. Standing charges also vary for different fuels and suppliers. Your energy supplier should explain these different tariffs and include them on your bills. There are many sources of information about cheapest energy prices that can be found on the internet; alternatively contact your nearest energy advice centre.

table 1.1 typical domestic fuel prices

Fuel	Lowest price (in pence/kWh)	Highest price (in pence/kWh)
Gas	2.05	4.02
Electricity (on-peak)	11.11	15.03
Electricity (Economy 7) – night rate	4.41	11.55
Oil (35 sec)	3.47	3.47
Coal	2.10	2.10
Wood pellets	2.80	4.17
Logs (broadleaf)	1.97	1.97

Source: Adapted from John Willoughby's Domestic fuel price guide, May 07 (see **www.johnwilloughby.co.uk**).

To get an approximate running cost of an appliance you can multiply the average annual kWh consumption figure supplied by the manufacturer (see energy label or user manual) by the price for a unit of electricity. Figure 1.3 shows an example of an appliance energy label.

For example:

An A-rated fridge-freezer with a predicted annual consumption of 325kWh at 10p/kWh for electricity would have an annual running cost of about £32.50 (325 × £0.10).

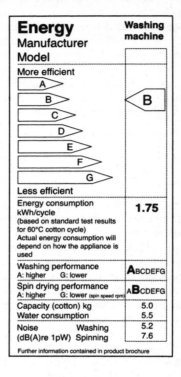

figure 1.3 example of an EU appliance energy label

What is Carbon?

You will regularly hear the terms 'Carbon emissions' and 'Carbon footprint' in relation to the environmental impact of energy use. The correct scientific term for what we are talking about is **carbon dioxide** or CO_2, which is released as we burn carbon-based fossil fuels, such as coal, oil and gas.

To assess the actual environmental impact of energy use, we measure the CO_2 released in kilograms ($kgCO_2$) or tonnes CO_2.

$$1 \text{ tonne } CO_2 = 1016 \text{ kgCO}_2$$

This is, in essence, the environmental currency for energy use.

Conversion factors are used to calculate the amount of carbon dioxide emitted per kWh by different fuels – see Table 1.2.

table 1.2 conversion factors for different fuels (Source: Energy Saving Trust, 2007)

Fuel type	kgCO$_2$/kWh
Natural gas	0.21
Grid electricity	0.53
Heavy fuel oil	0.26
Coal	0.35

For electricity, the real emissions vary year on year due to the different mix of fuels used in the power stations and are average grid figures – indeed they vary also at different times of the year and day. Grid electricity costs more financially and environmentally because of the poor efficiency (wastage) when converting fossil fuels in power stations to power that can be used in your home. Most of the losses occur at the power station itself as hot flue gases and steam in the cooling towers. Gas is much better as it is provided to the home after very little processing. This has important implications when deciding which energy efficiency measures you wish to introduce since some will be more worthwhile if you have an electric heating system rather than gas central heating.

Green tariff

'Green tariff' electricity is generated from renewable sources such as wind and sun. As a result, it does not produce any net CO_2 emissions. Switching to a supplier that can provide green tariff electricity can cut the average household's annual carbon footprint by two tonnes. However, green electricity is often more expensive and you could pay between 10 and 14 per cent more.

One important reason for opting for a green tariff, however, is to show energy suppliers that there is a demand for renewable energy and so support their investment in new technology and the expansion of this clean, low carbon energy supply.

02 how much energy are you using now?

In this chapter you will learn:
- where most energy is used in the home
- how to compare your energy use with others
- about Energy Performance Certificates and HIPs
- how the Energy Saving Recommended logo can help you
- what tools are available to assess your energy use
- how to use a carbon calculator.

The average homeowner

Domestic energy consumption has been steadily increasing over recent decades, despite many advances in technology to improve energy efficiency. This is partly due to greater expectations regarding personal comfort (such as wanting warmer homes) and to increasing numbers of appliances and gadgets that are deemed necessary in our modern lives to provide convenience and personal entertainment. Figure 2.1 illustrates our modern, energy-intensive lives.

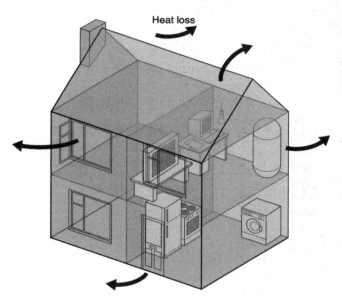

Heat loss

figure 2.1 a typical home! (© Hockerton Housing Project)

There are inevitably large variations in energy use between different types of properties. A compact, modern, well-insulated house with lots of 'A-rated' appliances will do considerably better than a large uninsulated Victorian home with older appliances, particularly if the occupants try and maintain similar levels of comfort. However, for the purposes of this book, the average homeowner is used, represented by a three-bedroom semi-detached property. You can then compare your annual energy use with the typical figures shown as a rough benchmark.

There are some basic 'rules of thumb' (reference Table 2.1):

- Space and water heating is responsible for the majority of energy used in the home, typically over 80 per cent (see also Figure 2.2).
- Homes heated by electric systems, rather than gas, produce far more carbon dioxide, as they are much less efficient at converting carbon into useful energy (see relative conversion factors, Table 1.2).
- Solid fuel heating systems use the largest amount of energy and carbon.

The amount of energy used for space heating and hot water as a proportion of total energy use is fairly similar for different sized properties, but the actual total usage does vary significantly.

table 2.1 estimated energy use and carbon dioxide emissions for main household uses for different space heating fuels (Source: Energy Saving Trust, 2007)

Fuel type for heating	Energy Use (kWh/yr)			Carbon dioxide use (kgCO$_2$/yr)		
	Space and water heating	Lighting and appliances	Cooking	Space and water heating	Lighting and appliances	Cooking
Gas central heating	21,200	3,000	1,300	4,452	1,590	<400
Electric storage heating	17,200	2,900	700	9,116	1,537	371
Oil heating	19,400	3,100	700	5,044	1,643	371
Solid fuel	31,100	3,000	700	10,885	1,590	371

Assumptions for table:

- Three-bedroom semi-detached properties.
- Energy use modelled using BREDEM-12 and assumes stock average dwelling characteristics, standard heating pattern and occupancy.

- Carbon dioxide conversion factor of:
  - Gas – 0.21 kgCO$_2$/kWh
  - Electricity – 0.53 kgCO$_2$/kWh
  - Oil – 0.26 kgCO$_2$/kWh
  - Solid – 0.35 kgCO$_2$/kWh

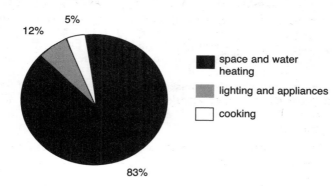

figure 2.2 breakdown of energy use by key usage type in a gas centrally heated property (from Table 2.1)

The proportion of electricity used by different electrical items in the home (excluding heating) is shown in Table 2.2.

table 2.2 relative electricity consumption in the home (excluding electric heating and hot water)

Use	Percentage of total use
Lighting	19
Electronics (e.g. TVs and toasters)	19
Cold appliances (fridges and freezers)	18
Cooking appliances	15
Wet appliances (e.g. washing machine)	15
ICT (e.g. computers and broadband services)	9
Others	5

How is my home officially rated?

Home energy ratings

Energy ratings tell you how energy efficient your home is. All new homes now have to have energy ratings applied to them in order to meet current Building Regulations (Part L). However, from late 2007, if you decide to sell your home you are likely to be required to have your house rated for an **Energy Performance Certificate** (EPC), as part of the new **Home Information Packs** (see below for further information about EPCs). Of course, if you are looking to purchase a home, the seller will be required to provide you with this valuable information.

There are two main energy ratings available within the United Kingdom:

- Standard Assessment Procedure (SAP)
- NHER rating.

SAP rating

This is the Government's recommended system for rating energy in homes. The SAP rating is based on energy costs for space heating, water heating, ventilation and lighting, less the cost savings from power generated by renewables. This means that it excludes the costs from cooking and electrical appliances. The rating is adjusted for floor area, and so it is independent of the size of homes.

A SAP rating is required for all new houses and those which are undergoing significant alteration, such as the addition of an extension. The latest version of SAP is SAP 2005, which has a scale of 1 to 100, 1 being very poor and 100 being excellent (zero energy costs!). A typical SAP rating for an average house in England is about 45. A SAP rating on a new house built to current Building Regulations should reach or exceed 80.

For more information about SAP see the website **http://projects. bre.co.uk/sap2005/**.

NHER rating

The NHER rating is more comprehensive than SAP since it takes into account the local environment and the effect it has on the building's energy rating. It also includes cooking, lights and appliances, and so provides a more detailed assessment of energy use than SAP. Indeed SAP was derived from NHER as a simplified version which could be calculated by hand.

The original NHER rating had a scale of 0 to 10, with 0 being poor and 10 being excellent. An average dwelling in England would score between 4.5 and 5.5. A newer house meeting current Building Regulations should reach or exceed 8.

The NHER scale has been recently extended up to 20, a score of which represents total fuel costs of zero – quite a challenge! Even to achieve a rating of 11 would require the dwelling to be generating some of its own electricity.

For more information about NHER see the website www.nher.co.uk.

Energy Performance Certificates (EPCs)

What are EPCs?

Energy Performance Certificates are an important part of the recently launched Home Information Packs (more commonly known as HIPs: see later for more information). An EPC informs prospective buyers about the energy performance of a house by providing the following:

- An **energy efficiency rating** – This is a measure of the overall efficiency of a home based on calculations using SAP (Standard Assessment Procedure) – see above. The higher the rating the more energy efficient the home is and hence the lower the fuel bills will be.
- The **environmental impact rating** – This is a measure of a home's impact on the environment in terms of carbon dioxide (CO_2) emissions. The higher the rating the less impact it has on the environment.

Figure 2.3 shows the A to G scale used, similar to that which you may be familiar with seeing on 'white goods' (such as your fridge). A is the highest rating and G the lowest. The EPC also indicates the potential for improvement and provides practical steps for reducing CO_2 emissions and costs.

For comparison, a home built to the 2006 Building Regulations would typically be around the boundary of bands B and C. However, the average property in the UK currently falls within bands D–E. Each rating is based on the performance of the building itself and its services, such as heating and lighting, and does not include the performance of the domestic appliances within it. The certificate also takes into account the age, location, size and condition of the building when providing a rating and suggesting improvements.

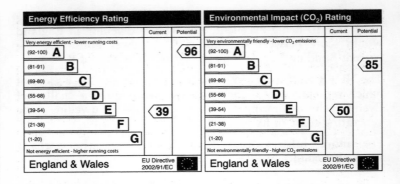

figure 2.3 example ratings chart from an Environmental Performance Certificate

You should pay particular attention to the following:

• These certificates may have a specific lifespan before they expire.
• The fuel costs only take into account the cost of fuel and not any associated service, maintenance or safety inspection costs.
• The certificate allows one home to be compared with another, but always check the date the certificate was issued. Since fuel prices can increase over time, an older certificate may under-estimate the property's fuel cost.

Will I be affected?

EPCs were launched in England and Wales as part of Home Information Packs for homes with four or more bedrooms being sold from 1 August 2007 and three-bedroom homes from 1 September 2007. This will be a requirement for other sized homes as it is rolled out in phases over the following 18 months, to include newly built homes and rented property. The Government expects that by 2010, over three million EPCs for homes will be required every year. EPCs can only be produced by trained and accredited Energy Assessors and Home Inspectors who will visit the property to collect the relevant data and create the certificate.

The Government provides information and guidance that explains the measures and how to apply them for home-sellers and buyers. You can find this guidance and more information at **http://www.communities.gov.uk/epbd**.

First results!

Following the introduction of Energy Performance Certificates (EPCs) for four-bedroom homes most are receiving a disappointing 'E' rating in their EPCs, but this could potentially rise to a 'C' if consumers undertake measures recommended in the certificates, like loft and cavity wall insulation.

The findings come from a snapshot survey of energy assessors and EPCs provided since their launch, which show average four-bed homes could typically save £180 on heating, £60 on lighting and £30 on hot water bills in a year.

The top five recommendations given by assessors for improving energy efficiency have been: cavity wall insulation, changing to low energy lighting, putting thermostatic valves on radiators, loft insulation, and double glazing. For more information see the website **www.homeinformationpacks.gov.uk**.

The benefits of EPCs

For the first time, homebuyers will have access to a clear indication of the relative energy use of one property versus another, which may well affect the house they select and how much they are willing to pay for it! The Government hope that EPCs will provide an opportunity to stimulate sellers' and buyers' interest in taking actions to improve energy efficiency such as improving insulation and heating in the property, either before or after purchase.

A high rating will benefit property **buyers** because it will specifically mean:

- lower energy bills immediately
- fewer actions required by owners in the medium to long term to improve energy efficiency, thereby saving further costs.

A high rating will benefit property **sellers** because it will:

- increase the marketability of their home, particularly as energy prices rise.

What is a Home Information Pack (HIP)?

A Home Information Pack, more commonly known as a HIP, includes a number of documents about a property being offered for sale. The packs are designed to ease the process of buying and selling houses by containing all the essential information about the property upfront, including an **Energy Performance Certificate**.

The packs contain both compulsory ('required') and optional ('authorized') documents. Compulsory documents:

• Home Information Pack Index
• Energy Performance Certificate
• Sales statement
• Standard searches (local authority enquiries, drainage and water search)
• Evidence of title.

It is expected that most estate agents will provide HIPs for little more than what it already costs for processing a sale, as it includes information such as searches which are already paid for in the current system. They may also be offered for free as part of a total package from estate agents, particularly with increased competition.

'Energy Saving Recommended' logo

The 'Energy Saving Recommended' logo (see Figure 2.4), developed by the Energy Saving Trust in conjunction with industry and Government, appears on a wide range of products including:

• insulation
• glazing
• gas boilers and heating controls
• kitchen appliances like fridges, freezers, dishwashers, washing machines and tumble dryers
• integrated digital televisions (IDTVs)
• light bulbs and light fittings.

However, the product range is continually expanding. Recently the logo has been used to endorse kettles, home computing and consumer electronic equipment.

Certification mark

figure 2.4 'Energy Saving Recommended' logo

It's your guarantee that these products are the most energy efficient in their category, will cost less to run and help prevent climate change. For example, for fridges, A+ models are endorsed which are more energy efficient than A rated products and washing machines must be AAA – that's A for energy, A for wash quality and A for spin.

The criteria is set by an independent panel and reviewed annually. In addition, a percentage of the products are tested so you can be assured that where there's a logo there's a smarter choice.

Products are also endorsed in categories where there isn't a statutory EU energy label, for example, glazing, televisions with integrated digital decoders (IDTVs) and boilers.

The idea is that whatever the product, whichever the labelling system, all you need to do is look for the Energy Saving Recommended logo.

The Energy Saving Trust website (**www.energysavingtrust. org.uk**) has a database which can be used to find a wide range of Energy Saving Recommended products with links to retailers' websites where you can then purchase – or call 0800 512 012 (free).

Energy self-assessment

How do you know if your home is wasting energy? Some waste is inevitable but for most households an energy efficiency survey is the first essential step towards identifying opportunities for making energy savings. You do not have to wait until you sell your home before assessing its energy efficiency, and once you can see the energy you are using and where it is going, you can start to make informed decisions. There are a number of resources available to help you make savings almost immediately.

Free energy audits

According to a 2007 report from the Institute for Public Policy Research, 'Positive Energy', providing every home with a free energy audit could lead to UK households saving up to £230 a year on their energy bills, as well as significantly reducing carbon dioxide emissions.

Home energy surveys

It is possible for you to employ an energy consultant to provide a formal survey and report. This could be similar to the work required for an Energy Performance Certificate, and could include consideration of your home's:

- heat loss
- construction
- heating (including controls)
- lighting
- insulation.

The advantage of paying for an independent professional assessment is that you will benefit from a great deal of expertise that may enable you to focus more quickly on the key areas for savings. They are also much more likely to spot areas for improvement and give you the confidence to take the necessary actions. Also, the fact that you have paid a fee may well act as an incentive to make changes and, if nothing else, recover the fee cost!

If you are feeling confident, however, and want to make your own assessment, then the following are examples of free resources available to help you survey your energy use. They will help you in planning your actions as you read through other parts of this book.

- **Energy Saving Trust 'Home Energy Check'** – By answering some simple questions about your home, the Energy Saving Trust will give you a free, personalized report telling you how you can save money on your household energy bills. Go to **www.energysavingtrust.org.uk** to find the survey, but if you would rather have a paper copy to complete, call 0800 512 012 and speak to your local Energy Saving Trust advice centre.

- **British Gas Energy Savers Report** – As part of the 'We're in this Together' campaign British Gas provides a free online energy efficiency audit. In 2006, 1.5 million customers completed the energy savers report on their home, and it is claimed that on average they are now saving around 10 per cent of their energy bills as a result of the energy efficiency measures they have implemented. The audit is based on 17 simple questions about your home and takes just a few minutes to complete. It provides a summary of the measures you could take to reduce your energy consumption and the savings that you would make as a result. It also tells you about the current and potential rating of your home on the A to G scale. Go to **www.house.co.uk/esr** to complete the report.

Technology assessment tools

There is an increasing amount of technology available to assist you in calculating where energy is being used in your home. These are useful not just for initial assessments, but also on an ongoing basis, to check how effective your actions have been in reducing energy use, and to facilitate fine tuning or a redirection of your efforts. The simplest and cheapest way of monitoring energy use is by using your electricity meter. Simply read your meter whilst somebody else puts on and off various household appliances to see which use the most electricity.

Single appliance energy monitors

There are a number of products available from DIY stores, green shops or even via 'Amazon' that are great for measuring how much energy individual appliances use. You can monitor the energy use in real time or the total consumption over a day or a week. They are very simple to use and understand – you just plug them into the socket with the plug from the appliance you are monitoring. The data is recorded and you can measure both energy use and cost. These energy monitors have the disadvantage, however, that you can only monitor one appliance at a time, and so it can take quite a while to get round the whole house and look at all your appliances. Also, they cannot monitor electricity used by appliances and lighting that connect directly into the mains.

They range in price from £10–£25, or you may be able to borrow one – The Norwich & Peterborough Building Society was offering customers in 2007 the opportunity to borrow a 'plug in' energy monitor!

Smart meters

A smart meter is a modern device which provides consumers with 'real-time' information about the energy they are using. This is a newly developing technology, ranging from simple bolt on additions to a basic meter, to advanced versions that communicate directly with energy suppliers. The Government says it expects everyone to have a smart meter within ten years and, as part of wider EU legislation, is currently considering forcing electricity suppliers to provide a real-time visual display unit to any new meters fitted from 2008, and to all households that request them between 2008 and 2010.

The benefits of smart meters include the following (see also, Figure 2.5):

- Real-time visual display units which can tell you how much energy you are using, and how much it is costing when appliances are turned on.
- The display can be placed in a more convenient location in the house for monitoring, such as the kitchen.
- More advanced meters can even control the amount of energy your house uses, for example, by turning off lights, or running appliances during periods of cheaper electricity.
- If you are considering microgeneration (see Chapter 05) smart meters will allow you to meter the energy you are generating and probably sell surplus back to the grid.

- More advanced smart meters will allow your energy suppliers to communicate directly with you, removing the need for meter-readings and providing accurate bills with no estimates.
- There is the potential for providing you with enhanced information on your bills to help you save energy, including historical comparisons of your energy use.

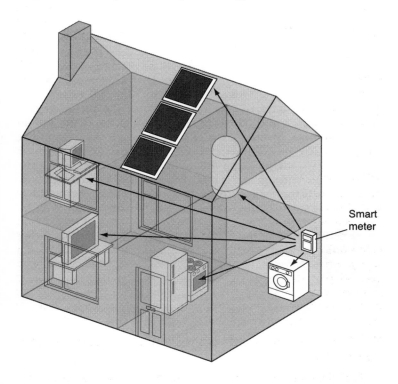

figure 2.5 diagram showing a potential smart meter set up (© Hockerton Housing Project)

The devices are simple to install, usually including a small sensor in your meter cupboard that measures how much energy you are using, and a small display that you can carry around the house. When you turn things on and off you can see the difference in how much energy you are using. You can immediately see the impact of your behaviour, not just in terms of money but in terms of carbon as well. Tests have shown savings of 13–25 per cent on electricity bills, and of approximately 250–500kg of carbon dioxide emissions per year.

Rather than wait for a smart meter to be installed as part of new legislation, you can go ahead now and purchase a smart meter, such as the 'Efergy' (see Figure 2.6) for less than £50. As the data on the screen of the Efergy meter is refreshed every five seconds, the impact on power usage of turning an electrical appliance on or off can be seen immediately. There is functionality to show data as total kW, pence per kWh, or emissions measured in terms of kg of carbon dioxide, $(kgCO_2)$. You can even set the meter to suit your own maximum kW consumption level so that an alarm will go off if this is exceeded. In addition, the Efergy meter also has a memory facility enabling the user to record total electricity usage on a daily basis which is then automatically recorded into the memory as a rolling weekly total. This can allow users to build up an accurate profile of their own electricity usage over time. The meter, the size of a standard domestic electric light switch, is easy to install, taking just a few minutes and not requiring any tools or cable-cutting, nor is it necessary to call in an electrician. Once set up, the transmitter has a range of 40 metres. It is available from the Efergy website at **www.efergy.com**.

figure 2.6 the Efergy smart meter

Carbon calculators

The amount of carbon dioxide emitted through the burning of fossil fuels by an individual, household, organization or even product is often referred to as their '**Carbon footprint**'. For an individual or household it refers to the emissions resulting from their daily activities. A carbon footprint for a product measures the emissions produced in the total process of the product reaching the market.

The amount of carbon you are personally responsible for in a year can be determined using a **carbon calculator**, with the carbon footprint often expressed as tonnes of carbon dioxide or tonnes of carbon produced. Your carbon footprint is broader than simply looking at your home energy use and usually covers your use of transport, in particular emissions from cars, and flying. Carbon calculators link your behaviour to your impact on the environment, in particular, climate change. Some calculators use your responses to create an individual 'Action Plan' showing you how to reduce your carbon footprint. Most calculators require basic data from users such as:

- the type of home you live in (e.g. detached or a flat)
- your main heating system (e.g. gas or electric)
- the types of appliances and gadgets you own and how you use them
- the type of car you own
- the number of flights you take per year.

If you can also provide information from your fuel bills, your final footprint calculation will be more accurate.

The objective of the calculators is not to give you an official energy rating of your home (this can only be done by a qualified assessor), but to act as an educational tool to help increase users' understanding of the impact of their behaviour on climate change. Information is often split into different key areas to help you identify where you could realize the most savings.

The things that are most likely to give you a higher than average footprint are as follows:

- If you/your family lives in a large or very old house then you are likely to use more energy for heating than an equivalent family in a modern or smaller house.
- If you have electric heating, rather than gas central heating, then electric heating is less carbon efficient.
- If you fly on a regular basis.

Problems with carbon calculators

Carbon calculators have some limitations, however:

- They use averages based on general models and simplified assumptions.
- It is difficult to take account of behavioural actions such as turning off appliances or turning down your central heating thermostat.
- They do not take into account different local climates which impact on energy use, particularly heating.
- They assume an energy mix for electricity based on the UK average.
- The majority of them only focus on a few key areas of your lifestyle.
- They generally only take into account direct emissions from those actions that we have control over, and do not take into account indirect ones, such as the manufacture and transport of products and food prior to purchase.

It is likely, however, that these calculators will become increasingly sophisticated and accurate as the demand for them increases.

Example carbon calculator – Act on CO$_2$

The 'Act on CO$_2$ calculator' (http://actonco2.direct.gov.uk/) was launched in June 2007 and is the first carbon calculator which uses Government-approved data. The Government wants it to become the gold standard for calculating CO$_2$ emissions from individuals and families.

'Carbonator' (http://www.carboncontrol.org.uk/carbonator/default.aspa) has been designed as a junior version.

Other carbon calculators

There are many other carbon calculators available. The ones listed below are not necessarily recommendations – why not try a few and find the one(s) that work best for you. They focus on different aspects of lifestyle and require different levels of input. Some are more user-friendly than others.

- Best Foot Forward: http://www.bestfootforward.com/carbonlife.htm
- Carbon Gym (by Centre for Alternative Technology): http://www.cat.org.uk/carbongym/
- Choose Climate: http://www.chooseclimate.org/flying/mapcalc.html

- Future Forests: **http://www.futureforests.com/acatalog/ indexworldcalculator.asp**
- Global Action Plan: **http://www.carboncalculator.org**
- International Council for Local Environmental Initiatives (ICLEI): **http://www3.iclei.org/co2/co2calc.htm**
- My Carbon Footprint: **http://www.mycarbonfootprint.eu/**
- The National Energy Foundation: **http://www.natenergy.org. uk/convert.htm**
- Safe Climate: **http://www.safeclimate.net/individual.php**
- Travel Calculator: **http://www.travelcalculator.org**
- WWF: **http://footprint.wwf.org.uk/**
- You Control Climate Change: **http://www.climatechange. eu.com/** (includes an opportunity for you to make a public pledge to reduce your personal carbon footprint).

Working with others

There are a number of organizations, often acting at a local level, which can provide householders with mutual support and guidance on making energy savings. Details of 'EcoTeams' and 'Carbon rationing action groups' are provided below, but if these are not available in your locality try contacting you local authority or energy advice centre to see if there are other options for you.

EcoTeams

EcoTeams are groups made up of six to eight households who commit to reducing their environmental impact from their energy and water use, their household waste, their transport and their consumer behaviour. By monitoring their habits and measuring improvements over a number of months, the households aim to change their behaviour and play their part in a cleaner, more sustainable future.

An EcoTeam is not simply a discussion group; it is a practical workshop where words and thoughts are translated into action. The work is shared by a group so that members can support and encourage one another and share experiences and ideas. It is a step-by-step process that helps people to change their lifestyle by small adjustments that become good habits. It takes surprisingly little time to get results – a couple of hours per month for group meetings and a few minutes measuring each week.

Anyone can form an EcoTeam – neighbours, friends, work colleagues or community groups such as pensioners, mothers, church groups and Women's Institutes. If you need advice about any aspect of the programme or if you would like to start an EcoTeam, email **ecoteams@globalactionplan.org.uk**. You can also visit the website: **www.ecoteams.org.uk**.

Carbon Rationing Action Groups

A Carbon Rationing Action Group (CRAG) is a group of people who have decided to act together to reduce their individual and collective carbon footprints. They do this on an annual basis. First they set themselves an annual emissions target or 'carbon ration'. Then they keep track of their emissions over the year by keeping a record of their household energy use and private car and plane travel. Finally, at the end of the year, they take responsibility for any emissions over and above their ration – their 'carbon debt'. All carbon debts are paid into the group's 'carbon fund' at an agreed rate per kilo of CO_2 debt. The fund is then distributed as agreed by the members of the group.

For more information see **www.carbonrationing.org.uk**.

03

developing a strategy for action

In this chapter you will learn:

- about the energy hierarchy
- why energy efficiency is the first priority
- how to develop action plans based on your energy-saving goals.

Don't be too put off by the many figures and statistics thrown about – including in this book – they are only estimates and averages. You can determine your own figures for your home and make it personal! By using monitoring and assessment tools and comparing before and after, you can calculate fairly accurately your own cost savings. If you want to convert these to CO_2 savings, you can do that as well, if you know your energy mix (see Chapter 01, 'What is Carbon?'). Of course you can never be absolutely sure about what you have saved, as you can't know exactly what you would have used if you had taken no action. However, the important thing is that you are doing something, however small, and it will make a difference to your costs and the environment.

Broad principles

Adopt the 'energy hierarchy'

The energy hierarchy, starting with the most energy effective actions, is a useful principle in helping you to make decisions about the order of actions needed to maximize the environmental benefit. Co-incidentally, it generally provides the most cost-effective approach as well. It is similar to the three 'Rs' principle for household waste – reduce, reuse, recycle. Figure 3.1 and Table 3.1 provide one way of developing an energy hierarchy model with examples.

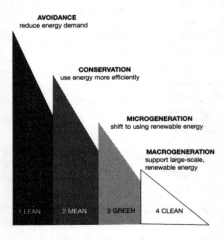

figure 3.1 the energy hierarchy (© Hockerton Housing Project)

Approach	Examples of actions
AVOIDANCE Reduce energy demand 'Be *lean*!'	• Turn down the central heating thermostat. • Don't leave appliances on stand-by. • Naturally ventilate rather than using air conditioning. • Walk rather than use the car.
CONSERVATION Use energy more efficiently 'Be *mean*!'	• Add insulation to reduce energy used for heating. • Upgrade from single to double glazing. • Upgrade to A-rated appliances. • Upgrade to an energy efficient boiler and controls. • Use low energy light bulbs. • Use public transport instead of the car.
MICROGENERATION Shift to using renewable energy 'Be *green*!'	• Use a solar thermal system for hot water. • Use a solar electric system (photovoltaics) to generate electricity. • Install a small wind turbine (Microwind). • Use a wood pellet stove.
MACROGENERATION Support large-scale, renewable energy 'Be *clean*!'	• Buy electricity on a 'green tariff' to reduce the burning of fossil fuels.

Conservation versus generation

Table 3.2 provides a more detailed consideration of two levels of the energy hierarchy described above; 'Conservation' and 'Microgeneration'. The examples in the table highlight that conservation measures generally have a much quicker payback than installing microgeneration technologies.

table 3.2 savings comparison between selected conservation and microgeneration actions (see Chapters 04 and 05 for details of assumptions used)

Action	Cost to install (£)	Annual energy savings (kWh)	Annual cost savings (£)	Payback (yrs)
CONSERVATION				
Replace five 60 Watt bulbs with low energy bulbs (15 Watt)	15	411	41	0.4
Cavity wall insulation	250	6,000	180	1.4
Draft proofing	90	714	18	5.0
GENERATION				
Photovoltaic (solar-electric) system (2.5kWp)	13,000	2,147	215–408	32–61
Solar hot water (4m²) – retrofit gas heated property	3,700	1,609	40	92

Choosing a strategy

Before you can decide on a strategy you need to understand your motives for energy saving. Your motives are likely to be one or a combination of the following:

• To save money.
• To reduce your impact on the environment.
• To improve the marketability of your house.

Chapter 01 covers these in more depth and reading this may help you decide where your motivation lies. You can then adopt the most appropriate strategy for you as follows:

1 Maximize cost-effectiveness.
2 Maximize environmental savings.
3 Maximize marketability.
4 Ease of implementation.

Maximize cost-effectiveness

What are the cost savings for different actions in the home?

You will no doubt have read and heard many claims about the potential cost savings to be made from taking energy-saving actions in the home. The figures given in this book to assist you in decision-making and planning are only a guide as there will be variability due to several factors:

- Differences in occupancy – Potentially the most variability will be due to the occupants, in terms of number, time spent in the house, age mix, interests and attitudes to energy saving.
- Different sizes and locations of houses – The estimates provided are for an 'average' UK home, usually based on a three-bedroom semi-detached property. A large, old Victorian house in Edinburgh will, of course, be very different from a flat in London.
- Different materials used in the construction of homes and for energy-saving measures, such as insulation products.
- Most homes use a mixture of fuels, such as gas and electricity, which have different costs.
- External factors such as energy price changes, material cost changes and weather (particularly affecting heating costs).

It is important, therefore, to check the notes and assumptions provided so that you can identify differences between the examples given and your own situation. Also, it is worth remembering that some of the benefits of energy-saving actions may be experienced as improved comfort – a warmer house for example.

Where data is available it has been provided as examples in tables at the end of most sections and then collated as a summary in appendices at the end of the book. The best way to determine how much you are saving is to compare your energy bills, before and after you have made energy-saving actions. It is more useful to look at like for like periods, for example, one spring quarter to another, and make notes of extreme situations, such as a harsh winter, as these may have a disproportional effect, particularly with heating costs. You could also look at reductions in energy use each time you make a change, using the various tools described in Chapter 02. From the energy savings you can then work out the cost savings for a year or longer.

Most of the energy-saving actions in the book have been categorized for convenience and to assist you in your planning as follows:

1 **No cost actions**

No cost measures generally involve changes in habits or behaviour, such as turning off a light switch. Hopefully, over time, they become second nature. They may also involve one-off actions, such as turning down the thermostat by 1 degree. Where there are many suggestions (such as under the section on 'Cooking') they have been further sub-divided in terms of how easy they are to achieve, e.g. whether they:

• are easy to do
• require some effort, or
• require more effort.

Most are small changes which you probably wouldn't even notice in practical terms but, over time, the savings add up for your household, and if repeated by many households in the UK and further afield, the impact would be considerable.

2 **Low cost actions**

These are not likely to cost more than £100 and in most cases a lot less, but generally provide a quick payback, and will help you make significant savings on your energy bills.

3 **Investment actions**

These generally cost hundreds, and in some cases thousands of pounds, particularly installing microgeneration systems. Although these measures require more investment of money and effort, there can be big cost savings and environmental benefits, particularly over the long term. Pay particular attention to payback figures.

Payback time!

As with any financial investment, the decision to spend a significant sum of money on an energy-saving feature needs to involve an assessment of the rate of return on that investment.

A payback calculation of how many years it will take to recoup the initial capital cost through the energy savings you will make is simple to do:

$$\text{Payback (number of years)} = \frac{\text{Capital cost } (\pounds)}{\text{Annual energy savings } (\pounds)}$$

(Note: This does not allow for loss of interest or loss of opportunity to invest in something else.)

However, care must be taken in estimating figures – predicted energy savings may not be as great as expected, particularly with renewable energy installations. It might be prudent to start with a few simple, low-cost actions that you can easily measure to gain confidence. You may even decide to roll forward your savings to invest in more significant steps. Table 3.3 provides examples of how different factors can impact on payback periods.

table 3.3 likely factors that will affect payback

Factor	Decrease payback (Improve return on investment)	Increase payback (Lower return on investment)
Energy prices	Increase in tariffs	Decrease in tariffs
Installation costs	Lower than expected, e.g. grant or other financial offer	Higher than expected
Maintenance	No downtime!	Non-budgeted maintenance costs
Product/material performance	Better than expected	Worse than expected
Lifespan of product/material	Higher than expected	Product failure or lower than expected
Weather	Colder weather than usual will decrease payback for actions that reduce heat loss	Warmer weather than usual will decrease payback for actions that reduce heat loss

Income generation (microgeneration only)	Payment received for exported energy and/or obtaining Renewable Obligation Certificates (ROCS)	No payment for exported energy and no ROCS received

Grants

There are grants and special offers available most of the time towards investing in energy-saving measures or microgeneration, which will provide you with an even greater incentive to take action. They reduce your financial risk and payback periods, so that cash savings add up even quicker. These will vary in terms of:

- **value** – This might be a percentage of total costs or a fixed sum or maximum amount. It is unusual to receive full funding, unless you are on income support, as they are generally incentives.
- **when they are available** – Many will run for defined periods of usually two to three years. Others maybe linked to a specific activity, such as when you move home. You may also need to be prepared to apply at specific times, such as the start of a month and to compete with others.
- **who can apply** – They may only apply to particular groups, such as those on income support, or community groups.
- **associated conditions** – There may be particular criteria as a condition of funding. For example, the Government funding of microgeneration in the UK requires householders to first install energy-efficiency measures such as low energy light bulbs.
- **how to apply** – This usually involves filling out forms, either on line or paper-based.

Check application guidelines and criteria very carefully before spending too long on applying. You do need to be prepared to fill out forms and be patient about approvals – however, help is often provided if you struggle with forms. You may also, in some circumstances, have to pay up front and then claim money back after with receipts. Finally, don't be fooled by offers that are more about making money for opportunistic companies, than saving you money. Make your own calculations, using this book as a guide, to check if any offer is really worthwhile. Government-backed schemes are usually very good and they often provide details of accredited installers and products.

Where appropriate, guidance has been given in this book on grants and special offers. However, the following are good general places to start looking:

- **Energy Saving Trust** (**www.est.org.uk** or phone 0800 512 012) – Provides independent advice and information about energy efficiency, insulation and renewable energy options, and the availability of grants. Call to find out what help, advice, grants and offers are available for your area.

- **DirectGov** (**www.direct.gov.uk**) – UK Government website that can be used to find contact details of your local authority and also useful to see what grants or special offers are available.

- **Home Heat Helpline** – (**www.homeheathelpline.org** or phone 0800 336699) – A free service offering practical energy advice for people concerned about paying their energy bills. Specially trained advisors can assist with applying for grants, provide advice on reducing energy bills, and finding company and Government benefits.

- **Utility companies** – Gas and electricity companies are already required by Government to help people reduce their energy use in the home, in particular for cavity wall and loft insulation. The discount usually ranges from 50 per cent to 100 per cent depending on whether you are in receipt of state benefits, and which type of benefit. Contact your local energy provider and, if they are not helpful, shop around. The following are worth a try:
  - British Gas
  - EDF Energy: 0808 101 4122 (**www.edfenergy.com**)
  - HEAT Cymru Project (Wales): 0800 093 40 50 (**www.heatproject.co.uk**)
  - Home Energy & British Gas: 0845 971 7731
  - Npower: 0800 022 220 (**www.npower.com**)
  - Powergen 0500 201 000 (**www.powergen.co.uk**)
  - Scottish Hydro Electric: 0845 777 6633
  - Scottish Power: 0845 601 7836 (**www.theenergypeople.com**).

- **Government funding for microgeneration** – There are a number of schemes available depending on where you are located in the UK, such as the 'Low Carbon Buildings Programme', that offer discounts of up to 50 per cent to install microgeneration technologies. See Chapter 05 for more details.

New green grants for homebuyers

A new system to help homebuyers get green grants worth hundreds of pounds to lower their fuel bills and make their homes greener was announced in August 2007, linked to the introduction of Home Information Packs (HIPs) and Energy Performance Certificates (EPCs). Most people are unaware that there are grants of £100 to £300 for loft and cavity wall insulation. Following talks with the Government, a number of major energy companies have agreed that when buyers move into their home and sign up to an energy contract they will get immediate access and information about 'green' grants or offers to consumers.

In addition, the scheme will include a new portal on the Energy Saving Trust's website (**www.est.org.uk**) where consumers only need to tap in their postcode to find details of offers available. Consumers who choose to give details from their EPC to suppliers will also receive targeted offers for recommendations in their certificate. The offers are funded by energy suppliers and other partners, with their investment in 'green grants' increasing to £2.5 billion over the next three years from April 2008, compared to £1 billion over the last three years.

Lowest financial risk ('cautionary approach')

If your main objective is to make cost savings at least risk, you will be interested in actions with little or no implementation costs, and least interested in investing in actions that have a long financial payback. The following priority order of steps is suggested for you:

- STEP 1: Use the **cheapest energy**
  - 'Shop around' different energy suppliers to see which is the least expensive for your type of usage. There are lots of resources available to help you to do this, many on the internet.
  - Change your usage patterns to take advantage of lower fuel tariffs, for example, use timers to operate appliances during 'off-peak' periods, such as at night.
- STEP 2: Implement as many **no cost** actions as possible
  - These are identified in Chapter 04.
  - Start with easy to do actions and gradually progress to those requiring more effort.
  - Calculate projected savings over a reasonable time period (three months to a year).

- STEP 3: Consider **low cost** actions (see Appendix 2).
  - These are identified in Chapter 04.
  - Use estimated savings from Step 2 to fund these actions and/or apply for appropriate grants/special offers.
  - Use **installation costs** and **payback** figures where provided to assess relative level of financial risk. Select those with lowest installation cost and shortest payback first.
  - Calculate projected savings over a reasonable time period (three months to a year).

- STEP 4: Consider **investment** actions (see Appendix 2)
  - These are identified in Chapters 04 and 05.
  - Use estimated savings/grants from Steps 2 and 3 to fund these actions.
  - Use **installation costs** and **payback** figures where provided to assess relative level of financial risk. Select those with lowest capital cost and shortest payback first.

See Table 3.4.

Maximize return on investment

If your main objective is to maximize your financial return, this will involve investment and, therefore, some risk. You will be interested in actions with the biggest profits, the 'big-hitters', but also with a good financial payback. You will be least interested in investing in actions that have a long financial payback and those that save only small amounts of money. The following priority order of steps is suggested for you:

- STEP 1: Use the **cheapest energy** (see above)

- STEP 2: Implement *selectively* **no cost** and **low cost** actions
  - These are identified in Chapter 04.
  - Focus on those actions that have obvious and significant cost savings. Lifetime saving estimates for many actions are provided in tables to assist you. Identify those with the highest **profits** by subtracting installation costs from lifetime savings.

- STEP 3: Consider **investment** actions
  - These are identified in Chapters 04 and 05.
  - Apply for all appropriate grants and special offers.
  - Calculate **profits** and **payback** figures to assess best returns. Select those with highest profitability and the shortest payback first.

See Table 3.5.

table 3.4 top five costed actions with lowest financial risk (see Appendix 2 for full list or individual topic sections in Chapter 04)

Action	Cost (£)	Annual financial savings (£)	Payback (yrs)	Lifespan of product (yrs)	Lifetime savings for action (£)
Insulation for hot water pipes – DIY	4	8	0.5	20	155
Fit radiator foil/panels	6	15	0.4	10	150
NEW hot water cylinder jacket (80mm) – DIY	12	18	0.7	15	269
Replace five 100 Watt bulbs with low energy bulbs (20 Watt)	15	73	0.2	10	730
Replace five 60 Watt bulbs with low energy bulbs (15 Watt)	15	41	0.4	10	411

Note: See tables in Chapters 04 and 05 for assumptions used and references for specific actions.

table 3.5 top five actions with greatest profitability (see Appendix 2 for full list or individual topic sections in Chapter 04)

Action	Cost (£)	Annual financial savings (£)	Payback (yrs)	Payback of product (yrs)	Lifespan savings for action (£)	Profit (lifetime savings less installation costs)
Internal wall insulation	1,500	311	4.8	30	9,323	7,823
External wall insulation (during wall repair)	1,900	311	6.1	30	9,323	7,423
Ground source heat pump (9kW system) – **off gas only**	12,800	885	14.6	20	1,7691	4,891
Adding 270mm loft insulation (no insulation to start with) – DIY	180	114	1.6	40	4,542	4,362
Adding 270mm loft insulation (no insulation to start with) – installer	500	114	4.4	40	4,542	4,042

Notes:

• Installing internal and external insulation – assumes single solid walls rather than cavity walls.

• Installing a ground source heat pump above is *only* for properties that cannot connect to mains gas, where the alternatives are electric, oil or coal-based heating systems. If you have access to mains gas, this could be one of the least profitable actions.

• See tables in Chapters 04 and 05 for assumptions used and references for specific actions.

Maximize environmental savings

To assess the actual environmental impact of energy use, we measure $kgCO_2$ or tonnes CO_2 (1 tonne CO_2 = $1016kgCO_2$). These measures are, in essence, the environmental currency for energy use.

In general any savings in energy costs will mirror reductions in emissions of CO_2. Therefore, you would expect to have a similar strategy if you want to reduce your impact on the environment as the strategy to make cost savings. However, two key factors make a difference:

1 **Carbon intensity of fuels** – Use of different fuels in the home are associated with widely varying amounts of carbon dioxide emissions. This is particularly significant when comparing gas and electricity (for more details see Chapter 01, 'What is Carbon?').

   This means, for instance, that actions to reduce electricity use have a far greater impact on reducing CO_2 emissions (more than double) than actions to reduce gas use. For example, a kWh saved by an energy efficient fridge, will save more CO_2 than a kWh saved by adding more insulation in a gas heated home. This does not necessarily mean reduction of electricity should take a priority over reduction of gas – just that it needs to be factored in when making environmental decisions.

2 **Embodied energy** – This is the energy used to manufacture, transport, install, maintain and decommission a product or material. This can be a significant amount and so could reduce the overall environmental benefit of some energy-saving actions. Embodied energy figures have not been factored in to the CO_2 figures provided in action tables. However, some general rules of thumb are:

   • behavioural changes (e.g. turning lights off) are more environmentally beneficial than indicated, as they clearly do not have any associated embodied energy (especially if you discount the energy used to get up and turn the light off!).

   • insulation materials and low energy light bulbs have a relatively low embodied energy compared to the energy they save in the long term.

- upgrading old boilers and appliances also usually gives a quick payback of embodied energy.
- microgeneration technologies have a relatively high embodied energy and so some products need several years to generate enough CO_2 savings to offset their embodied energy.

Lowest risk

If your main objective is to make carbon dioxide (CO_2) savings at least risk, you will be interested in actions with little or no implementation costs combined with low embodied energy, and least interested in investing in actions that have a long financial payback and microgeneration technologies. The following priority order of steps is suggested for you:

- STEP 1: If you are not doing so already, think about **using gas for heating, hot water and cooking**, particularly if you are currently using electricity (gas has a much lower carbon intensity).

- STEP 2: Implement as many **no cost** actions as possible
  - These are identified in Chapter 04.
  - Start with easy to do actions and gradually progress to those requiring more effort.

- STEP 3: Consider **low cost** actions
  - These are identified in Chapter 04.
  - Use **cost (£) per tonne of** CO_2 saved (where provided) to guide you.

- STEP 4: Consider **investment** actions
  - These are identified in Chapters 04 and 05.
  - Use **cost (£) per tonne of** CO_2 saved (where provided) to guide you.
  - Only consider installation of microgeneration (renewable energy systems) once you have completed most, if not all relevant conservation actions and if you are reasonably sure they are going to perform to expectation.

See Table 3.6.

table 3.6 top five environmental – lowest risk actions (see Appendix 2 for full list or individual topic sections in Chapter 04).

Action	Cost (£)	Annual financial savings (£)	Payback (yrs)	Lifespan of product (yrs)	Annual CO_2 savings (kg)	Lifetime CO_2 savings for action (tonnes)	£ spent/tonne CO_2 saved
Insulation for hot water pipes – DIY	4	8	0.5	20	65	1	3
Replace five 100 Watt bulbs with low energy bulbs (20 Watt)	15	73	0.2	10	387	3.8	4
Adding 270mm loft insulation (no insulation to start with) – DIY	180	114	1.6	40	950	37	5
NEW hot water cylinder jacket (80mm) – DIY	12	18	0.7	15	150	2	5
Fit radiator foil/panels	6	15	0.4	10	105	1.0	6

Notes:

• Similarity with 'lowest financial risks' (see Table 3.4).

• See tables in Chapters 04 and 05 for assumptions used and references for specific actions.

Maximize environmental savings

If your main objective is to maximize the amount of CO_2 saved, this will involve investment for some actions and, therefore, some risk. The following priority order of steps is suggested for you:

- STEP 1: If you are not doing so already, **use gas for heating, hot water and cooking,** particularly if you are currently using electricity (gas has a much lower carbon intensity).

- STEP 2: Implement as many **no cost** actions as possible
  - These are identified in Chapter 04.
  - Start with easy to do actions and gradually progress to those requiring more effort.

- STEP 3: Consider **low cost/investment** actions
  - These are identified in Chapters 04 and 05.
  - Use CO_2 **reductions** (where provided) to assess relative effectiveness.
  - Only consider installation of microgeneration (renewable energy systems) once you have completed most, if not all relevant conservation actions and if you are reasonably sure they are going to perform to expectation.

See Table 3.7.

table 3.7 top five environmental – maximum savings actions (see Appendix 2 for full list or individual topic sections in Chapter 04)

Action	Cost (£)	Annual financial savings (£)	Payback (yrs)	Lifespan of product (yrs)	Annual CO_2 savings (kg)	Lifetime CO_2 savings for action (tonnes)	£ spent/ tonne CO_2 saved
Ground source heat pump (9kW system) – **off gas**	12,800	885	14.5	20	4,688	92.3	139
Internal wall insulation	1,500	311	4.8	30	2,600	77	20
External wall insulation (during wall repair)	1,900	311	6.1	30	2,600	77	25
Small wind – mast mounted (5–6kW) +ROCs	17,500	850	21	25	2,372	58.4	300
Adding 270mm loft insulation (no insulation to start with) – DIY	180	114	1.6	40	950	37	5

Notes:

• Installing a ground source heat pump above is *only* for properties that cannot connect to mains gas, where the alternatives are electric, oil or coal-based heating systems. If you have access to mains gas, the environmental benefits are considerably lower.

• See tables in Chapters 04 and 05 for assumptions used and references for specific actions.

Maximize marketability

The growing public awareness of the financial and environmental costs of energy use means that a more energy-efficient house is potentially more attractive to purchasers.

The recent introduction of Home Information Packs, which includes the requirement for an Environmental Performance Certificate (see Chapter 02) will provide potential purchasers with a clear assessment of the relative energy use of your property versus others. This is an opportunity to 'show off' improvements you have made, increase your chance of getting a quick sale and potentially increase the sale value.

Simple things you can do to improve the energy efficiency will be more cost effective in attracting buyers, rather than showing off the latest fancy green gadget. Evidence indicates that your priorities should be:

- being able to demonstrate low running costs through energy bills and an Environmental Performance Certificate
- ensuring good levels of insulation, double glazing and low energy lighting
- ensuring the boiler is in good condition and working efficiently.

In contrast, things that are less likely to attract buyers are:

- microgeneration technologies
- ecologically friendly building materials
- rainwater harvesting.

Ease of implementation

Your strategy may be to focus on those actions that you can implement yourself and continue to do so over a long period. This may require certain skills for some installations, but investing in DIY training may be worthwhile if it saves you significant installation costs.

You will need to bear the following in mind:

- **Health and safety** – Make sure you have the correct protective gear and your installation does not cause in-use health issues.
- **Accessibility** – How easy is it for you to access the relevant parts of the house where the measure is to be installed?
- **Physical ability** – How physically able are you to carry out the measures?
- **Human resources!** – Number of people required to fully install a measure. Who is available to help you (e.g. friends, family, neighbours)?
- **Time required** – Do you have enough time allocated to do the job properly?
- **Tools and materials** – Make sure you have the right tools and materials available and to hand when you are ready for installation.

The following priority order of steps is suggested for you:

- STEP 1: Implement as many **no cost** actions as possible
  - These are identified in Chapters 04, 06 and 07.
  - Start with easy to do behavioural actions and gradually progress to those requiring more effort and practical skills.

- STEP 2: Consider **low cost/investment** actions
  - These are identified in Chapters 04 and 05.
  - Start with those actions you feel most competent to do yourself and gradually progress to those requiring more effort and practical skills. Table 3.8 gives an idea of relative ease of action, where 1 is least complex and 5 is most complex.

table 3.8 relative ease of action for different measures

Measure	Ease of action
Substitute light bulbs with low energy types	1
Installation of hot water cylinder jacket	1
Upgrade appliances to A-rated models	1
Upgrade heating controls (TRVs)	1
Draught stripping	1
Cavity wall insulation	2
Top-up loft insulation	2
Upgrade boiler to more efficient condensing model	3
Full double glazing	4
Floor insulation	4
Install solar hot water heating	4
Install photovoltaic panels	4
Install a biomass heating system (wood boiler)	4
Erect a wind turbine	5
Install a ground source heat pump system	5

Putting strategy into action

The steps outlined below serve as a process which you can follow as you move from initial motivation, through decision-making, planning and implementation.

1 **Understand the subject, the problems and opportunities** – Try and read the whole of this book first!
2 **Define your motives** (see Chapter 01):
   • Saving money.
   • Reducing environmental impact.

- Selling home.
- Ease of installation.

3 **Benchmark** – Understand your starting point by assessing how energy efficient you are currently (see Chapter 02).

4 **Assess your resources:**

- **Financial:**
  - Decide what savings you are willing to use. You could roll forward savings from some energy-efficiency actions for greater investments.
  - Check if you can obtain grants or other financial support.
  - If you plan to borrow, check what loans are available.
  - Create a budget – This does not need to be exact, initially it could just be a ball park figure of what you are willing to invest.
- **Practical skills** – Write a list, but be honest. How much can you do yourself, and where will you need professional help? Can you draw upon friends, neighbours, family to help, particularly if they have relevant qualifications or experience?
- **Time availability** – Again, be honest and realistic. How much time can you put into this? Are you able to use evenings, weekends or take time off work? When will be the best time to do things – summer/winter, when the family are away?

5 **Create an action plan** – This can be as simple or complex as you want but here are some general rules:

- Make sure it is realistic and achievable.
- Get support for your plan, where relevant, from all house occupants, including partners, children (especially teenagers!) and lodgers.
- Start with simple measures; otherwise you may scare/put off others in the house.
- Don't set your expectations and targets too high, you may end up becoming de-motivated if all does not go to plan.

A simple plan could be just a job list. A more complex plan could look something like Table 3.9.

6 **Maintenance** – For those actions that require ongoing effort, you may wish to create some sort of work plan. This will vary, of course, depending on the type of action. For example, you could create posters or daily tick sheets for behavioural

actions such as turning off lights and appliances. For installations requiring maintenance you could create a log book rather like a car log book, to record dates and actions, notes of problems and how they were resolved.

table 3.9 action plan template

Task	Who to action	Target date to complete	Budget	Actual cost	Projected savings (£)	Projected savings (CO$_2$)	Follow up
Top up loft insulation	Dad	Dec 08	£50	£60	Look up tables	Look up tables	Check in a year
Change five traditional light bulbs to low energy ones	John	Sept 07	£10	£12	Look up tables	Look up tables	Replace another five in 6 months

04 energy saving in the house

In this chapter you will learn:
- measures to reduce space heating energy use, but stay warm
- how to manage hot water more effectively
- ways to use less electricity in the kitchen
- actions to control the growing electronic menace
- about low energy lighting
- how to stay cool more efficiently
- ways to manage teenage consumers
- what to do when moving home.

Keeping warm (heating)

For centuries open fires were our only form of domestic heating. Inefficient and wasteful, their only benefits were the radiant heat from burning fuel and some milder warmth from heated chimneys. Nowadays, they are mainly used as attractive focal points in homes heated by more modern means. In more recent years there has been a growing market for heating homes and water by burning wood or wood-based products (biofuels), through more efficient means – see Chapter 05, 'Generating your own energy'.

Over 90 per cent of UK homes are kept warm and comfortable through **central heating systems**. This allows the heating of many rooms from one source that is much more efficient and easier to maintain. Central heating systems can be divided into two main types:

- **Wet systems** using the medium of water.
- **Dry systems** using heated air to carry warmth to rooms.

Choice of fuel

The use of different types of fuel for heating systems makes a big difference to energy costs and environmental impact. Gas central heating costs are a half to two thirds of those of electric heating, typically 2.5p versus 10p per kWh. The carbon emissions of gas systems per unit of energy (CO_2/kWh) are also less than half those of electric systems. It is no surprise, therefore, that by 2003, 93 per cent of UK household's had gas central heating.

The big hit!

The modern central heating system has allowed homeowners to be much more in control of their indoor environment, fine-tuning their thermal comfort levels.

However, heating has become by far the most significant portion of energy use in UK homes, ranging from 50–80 per cent (see Figure 2.2).

The greatest potential, therefore, for energy and cost savings in the home will be derived from improving the efficiency of heating systems.

Space heating standards and systems have improved over the last decade, facilitating upgrades with more efficient heating and finer controls. Today most homes are fitted with loft insulation and the thickness has been improving as homeowners realize the benefits. Although some of these upgrades can be costly, they can often be tied in with general home improvements. It is important, however, to recognize that significant energy savings can also be achieved through simple behavioural changes and small inexpensive improvements.

The basics of a wet central heating system

Wet systems are by far the most popular form of central heating. Water is heated by a boiler and pumped through small-bore pipes to radiators or convector heaters where the heat from the water is released into the rooms. The water circulates back to the boiler for reheating in a continuing cycle.

This is a very flexible system allowing heat output from individual heaters to be adjusted via thermostats and valves. An extra advantage of a wet system is that it can also heat hot water for the home. The boiler may be fuelled by gas, oil, bottled gas, solid fuel or electricity (immersion).

New boilers, radiators and controls have been developed over recent years that have greatly improved energy efficiency. The overall effectiveness can be greatly improved by two key features:

1 A **high-efficiency boiler** minimizing waste heat (more information later in this chapter).
2 **Good controls** to ensure that the boiler only operates when heat is required. These include:
   • an electronic timer or programmer
   • a room thermostat
   • thermostatic radiator control valves (TRVs)
   • separate thermostatic control on the hot water system.

The timer or programmer

The programmer allows you to set your heating to suit your lifestyle. It automatically controls the times at which your central heating system switches on and off. Common features include the following:

• Seven-day functionality allows you to set different heating patterns for weekdays and weekends if necessary.

- Some timers allow different patterns for each day of the week which is particularly useful for those working part-time or on shifts that vary from the conventional Monday–Friday work pattern.

- Some programmers incorporate built-in thermostats and temperature sensors which need to be sited in a living room rather than by the boiler.

- Many programmers have an 'override/advance' button that is useful for exceptional situations, such as coming home early or sudden changes in weather. It allows you to override the programmer and switch the heating on or off early.

The room thermostat

The thermostat controls the temperature of your whole home based on the temperature of the circulating air. If the air temperature is at or above the set level it stops the boiler from operating the central heating and the radiators will then cool down. When the air temperature cools below the set level of the thermostat, it sends another signal to the central heating boiler to start heating up water again and to pump it around your pipes to your radiators, which then warm up once more. Room thermostats are usually found in the living room, hallway or dining room.

Thermostatic radiator control valves (TRVs)

Thermostats can also be fitted to the radiators themselves. They allow you to finely control the heating by switching individual radiators on or off depending on the temperature in each room.

Thermostatic controls on the hot water system

Some older systems only allow the heating to run when the hot water is on and this can be quite wasteful of fuel. It is more efficient if the hot water can be controlled by the programmer separately from the central heating. There should also be a separate thermostat on the hot water tank strapped to the outside near the bottom which controls the water temperature and it should not normally be set higher than 60°C.

Dry central heating systems

The heat source for most warm-air central heating systems is a large electric storage heater that contains a quantity of firebricks with electric heating elements running through them. The system takes advantage of cheaper off-peak electricity supply available during the night to heat the bricks, and the bricks release their heat slowly during the day. A fan blows the warm air through ducts to the rooms being heated. Controls are used to regulate the heat emissions and hence temperature within rooms. Storage heaters are frequently used in areas where there is no gas supply.

The ducted warm-air system is the only dry heating system that is genuinely central, that is, with a central heat source. A house heated by individual storage heaters, although generally regarded as centrally heated, is in fact heated by several separate heat sources.

Alternative heating systems

Heated floors

Heated floors have been around for some time now. They work either via electric cables within the flooring itself, or by running hot water through pipes in the floor. The whole heated floor area acts as a low temperature emitter. These systems have been much improved since the 1960s when they were first installed and early problems have been rectified.

High performance stoves

These stoves can be up to 80 per cent efficient (i.e. 80 per cent of the heat is used to heat the air space rather than going up the chimney or flue) compared to traditional wood stoves at about 40 per cent efficiency. Open fires are even worse at only 10–15 per cent efficiency. Modern high performance stoves have been developed in North America and Scandinavia – they use masonry to absorb and release heat over long periods, not unlike the way storage radiators work with bricks. This provides a more even radiant heat.

Wood chip and pellet burners are a relatively recent innovation and there are also models available for burning sawdust and wood shavings. Wood chips and pellets are more expensive than logs, but provide more heat by weight.

See Chapter 05, 'Generating your own energy' for further details under Biofuels.

No cost actions

Easy to do:

- Turn your thermostat down. A reduction of just 1°C could cut your heating bills by up 7.5 per cent and save you about £50 per year.

What temperature to keep the house?

As you lower the settings for internal temperature, the energy consumed falls significantly – at least 10 per cent for each degree (for the first few degrees). Reducing the temperature of the space and water heating in your home significantly could save almost half of your household energy consumption.

The average internal temperature of UK homes is about 21°C, two degrees higher than the current regulations which recommend a temperature of 19°C. Although 18–21°C may be fine for a living room, it is in most circumstances too high for a bedroom where 15–17°C is sufficient and, in fact, far better for your health. Higher temperatures dry out the nasal passages and can prevent a good night's sleep. However, if you are a pensioner or infirm then you may wish to set it higher, such as 21–24°C.

Keep circulation spaces (hall and stairs) cool (e.g. 11°C) although it is worth having some heating in them or every time a door is opened it can cause problems with the main thermostat being untimely triggered.

Where should I locate the thermostat?

Avoid placing thermostats in areas prone to draughts or too close to heat emitters and keep them out of direct sunlight. They are best located in a living room rather than the hallway as the hall temperature can be affected by the front door being used. They should ideally be fixed 1.2–1.8m above the floor.

- Turn the thermostat right down when you are going away on holiday or are going to be absent from your house for any length of time. A setting of only 5°C will still prevent pipes bursting in extreme cold weather.
- Set your heating to come on about half an hour before you want your home warm (usually before you get up and when you come home in the evening), and to go off about half an hour before you go out or go to bed. Ideally it should be run for two periods a day and not for more than nine hours per

day in total. It is not true that boilers work best when left to run continuously or that you save energy by having the heating on all day.

- Close your curtains at dusk during cooler/cold periods of the year to reduce heat escaping through the windows.
- Open the curtains if it is sunny during cooler/cold periods of the year to let the sun heat your room.
- Tuck curtains behind radiators to allow the heat from the radiator into the room. If curtains are allowed to hang over radiators the heat is funnelled out to the window.
- Keep furniture away from radiators or other heaters to allow heat into the room.
- Leave your oven door open after you have used it for cooking, the warm air will help heat your home.
- Close internal doors when the heating is on to reduce draughts.

Some effort:

- Leave hot water in the bathtub or in cooking pots (covered to avoid adding to room humidity) instead of draining it immediately. The water's stored heat will dissipate into your home rather than being lost down the drain.
- Keep all south-facing windows especially clean to maximize light and heat gain.
- Block up unused fireplaces to prevent heat being lost up the chimney. You can use scrunched-up newspaper packed into the hole where the fireplace enters the chimney, or buy special balloons. These still allow some air to circulate to avoid damp.

More effort:

- Put a jumper on! Putting on an extra layer or wearing warmer fabrics is a very efficient means to keep warm. Is it sensible to walk around the house in winter in a T-shirt with the heating on full blast?
- Bleed trapped air from hot-water radiators regularly. Sometimes air gets trapped inside the radiator. If this happens, the top of the radiator will feel cold whilst the bottom of the radiator will be warm.

Bleeding radiators!

Care is needed when bleeding radiators as there is a risk of scalding and damage to decor and carpets. Turn the heating OFF for a while before you begin, to avoid being scalded and ensure that your decor and carpets are carefully protected.

To bleed the radiator, open the valve at the topside of the radiator very slowly, with a radiator key, until all of the air has escaped. Have a bowl handy to catch any water that escapes from the radiator – it can be very dirty and therefore could stain.

If you have a combination (combi) boiler there will be a dial on the front of your boiler which measures the pressure in 'bars'. A heating contractor will need to bleed the radiator for you.

Doing this at least once a year will improve your heating efficiency.

How to set up storage heaters more efficiently

The basic principle of storing and releasing heat is common to all storage heaters, though the names of the controls may change from appliance to appliance. There are two basic controls for storage heaters:

1 Input Control (sometimes called Charge or Auto-set Control)
This dial controls the amount of heat that is charged into the unit during the off-peak hours and, therefore, the amount of electricity the unit will use. The dial usually has a scale of 1–6 and you will need to adjust the setting to meet your heating needs. Once you have determined how much heat you require the unit to take in during the charge period, the dial should be left on the desired setting.

2 Output Control (sometimes called Boost or Room-temperature Boost)
This dial controls the heat that is released from the unit and, similarly, usually has a scale of 1–6. When it is turned up, a flap opens on the insulated section of the unit and releases the stored heat, much like opening an oven door. You should adjust the dial to the lowest setting just before you go to bed so that heat being charged into the unit over night will not be released before it is needed. The dial should also be adjusted to the lowest setting when you leave the house so that heat is not released into an empty property.

The output dials can be adjusted throughout the day to release the heat as needed and should be fully open by last thing at night. The aim is to set the 'input' dial to a level that allows enough heat to be charged into the unit to last until you go to bed, and no more. By the time you go to bed, the heaters should be cold having provided sufficient heat to last the evening. This way you are not paying for stored heat you are not using. (Source: Tipthe planet – **www.tiptheplanet.com.**)

Savings summary

table 4.1 financial and environmental savings (keeping warm – no cost actions)

Action	Annual cost savings (£)	Annual energy savings (kWh)	Annual CO_2 savings (kg)
Reduce the temperature of your home by 1°C	40	1,600[1]	336
Reduce the temperature of your home by 3–4°C	108	4,300[1]	903
Programme the thermostat of your home lower by 3°C for 12 hours per day at night or when you're out of the house	53	2,095	440[2]

Notes:

- Assume $0.21 kgCO_2/kWh$ for gas consumption at a cost of 2.51p/kWh. If you have an electric-based heating system, the environmental and cost savings would be two–three times greater.
- [1]Typical three-bed semi-detached gas-heated home uses 16,000 kWh per annum for space heating (Source: Energy Saving Trust). Assume 10 per cent energy saved for first degree centigrade of reduced temperature and then a lower percentage for further reductions (various sources).

- $^2CO_2$ emission savings – Source: **www.mycarbonfootprint.eu** (calculator produced by European Commission – the calculator clearly defines the assumptions for figure).

Low cost actions

Fit draught excluder to letterbox

For a few pounds you can plug that hole, or at least cut out most of the draughts. To do it at no cost, simply tack a light plastic sheet or piece of carpet over the inside. Remember to check that the postman can still get your post through! Alternatively, block in the letterbox completely (and insulate) and replace with an external mailbox.

Install radiator foil

If you have radiators against external walls, up to 70 per cent of the heat will be lost to the wall, particularly if your walls are not insulated. This heat loss can be very easily and cheaply reduced by putting silver foil behind these radiators (see Figure 4.1), which reflects the heat back into the room. But don't do this for radiators against internal walls, as it will make no difference.

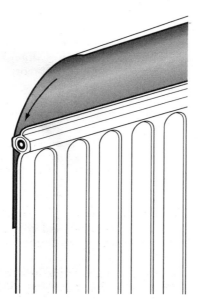

figure 4.1 radiator foil

Practicalities (radiator foil):

- You can buy specific products for this (from B&Q for example), which have a layer of insulation incorporated with aluminium foil.
- If you are retrofitting foil with radiators already installed, you should cut the foil to a size slightly smaller than the radiator and attach with adhesive pads. Otherwise paste the foil onto the wall before the radiator is fitted.
- It is possible to use ordinary kitchen foil but this is less effective.
- For radiators on internal walls it maybe worth painting the wall behind it with a dark colour to facilitate greater absorption of heat into the wall behind it. This uses the thermal mass of the house to keep a more even room temperature.

Line curtains

Line your curtains with thick, fluffy materials such as brushed cotton or wadding to help retain heat. Specially designed thermal curtains are available which provide extra insulation and you can even buy curtains with a reflective backing that reflect heat back into the room.

Draught proofing (Draughtstripping)

The uncontrolled entry of cold air, usually from around poorly fitting doors, windows and floors, creates draughts. Draughts mean that warm air is escaping from these points. According to the Energy Saving Trust, 20 per cent of all heat loss in a typical home is through ventilation and draughts (although some will be necessary ventilation). Draughts also create discomfort which often results in you turning the heating up to compensate. So by excluding draughts, you not only reduce heat loss from your home, but you are also more likely to turn the heating down in general.

Safety first!

Whilst draught excluders help to prevent heat loss, they also stop fresh air from entering. In rooms housing boilers (especially gas appliances without a balanced flue) or fires, controlled ventilation is necessary to prevent accumulation of dangerous gases such as carbon monoxide. Ventilation is also necessary in areas prone to dampness such as kitchens and bathrooms. A balance between cutting out draughts and providing enough ventilation can be achieved through the use of adjustable ventilators such as trickle vents in window frames and extractor fans in areas likely to have condensation problems. Chimneys should be swept regularly and air bricks checked for blockages.

Practicalities (draught proofing):

- Draught proofing is an easy, cost-effective DIY task that will reduce heating bills. Most materials are available from DIY stores. Check that they conform to the standard BS 7386 as the quality of the products will affect their performance and durability.

- A wide variety of excluders are available. Simple self-adhesive foam strips are inexpensive and suitable for windows and interior doors (see Figure 4.2). Make sure that they are not stretched when fitted as this will impair efficiency. Unfortunately, they generally only last a couple of years before they become permanently compressed. Polypropylene tubes are a little more expensive but will last longer and are more effective.

- A quick and cheap way to reduce heat loss from windows is to apply secondary glazing film.

- For external doors you can fit a threshold excluder if draughts are coming in. You can use rubber or brush strips or, alternatively, two-part excluders where one part is fixed to the door and the other to the threshold – when the door is closed, the two parts interlock to form a tight seal. You can also buy complete door sets for external and internal doors.

- Rubber draught strips and brush seals come in a variety of finishes to blend with existing woodwork or door/window hardware.

- Don't forget to fit key hole covers over keyholes and draught excluders over letterboxes.

- Check what grants and offers are available to help you pay for draught proofing – see Energy Saving Trust website (**www.energysavingtrust.org.uk**) or call 0800 512 012 (free).

figure 4.2 draught proofing window with self-adhesive foam strip

Fit thermostats to radiators

Thermostats can also be fitted to the radiators themselves. These are known as thermostatic radiator control valves (TRVs) and are fitted on the pipe-work at the top or bottom of the radiator (see Figure 4.3). They allow you to finely control the heating by switching individual radiators on or off depending on the temperature in each room. Radiators in rooms that aren't in use can be turned off completely. Each TRV can be set to a separate temperature, so you can have different temperatures in different rooms.

Practicalities (TRVs):

- TRVs are not expensive and you can fit them yourself if you are comfortable with plumbing.
- If you already have TRVs fitted, check them for maximum sensitivity and replace them if necessary.
- TVRs are marked with a * and numbers from 1 to 5. The * setting protects against frost and it will typically leave the radiator switched off unless the temperature falls below about 6°C. For a normal living room, the setting of 3 or 4, corresponding to about 20°C (68°F) should be about right. For bedrooms, a cooler temperature will normally suffice.

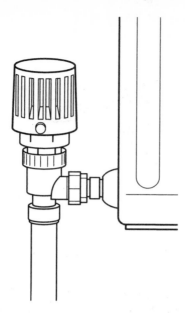

figure 4.3 thermostatic radiator control valve (TRV)

If you need to adjust the temperature in the room, turn the TRV up or down by one notch. Do not turn the TRV fully ON or fully OFF to make the room you are in warmer or cooler as this will waste fuel. Turn it a little way at a time and let it do the work.

• Sometimes there needs to be one or more radiators in your home which does not have a TRV so that it is always open to allow water to flow into it if the others are turned off. This avoids damage to the pump or boiler. You should not have a TRV on the radiator which is in the same room as the main thermostat, as if it turns the radiator off at a lower temperature, it can mislead the main thermostat into thinking that the house is cooler than it really is.

More advanced heating controls

There are a number of more advanced controls now on sale.

Intelligent heating controllers

Intelligent heating controllers such as the 'Dataterm', give the very best control over central heating, although they cost somewhat more than normal controls. They adjust the heating to take into account the length of time it takes the house to heat up in different weather conditions. They also often allow for different temperatures to be set for day and night.

Weather compensators

These replace a normal room thermostat and measure either internal or external temperature. They can then delay switching on the central heating on milder days. Simple ones are quite inexpensive and are well worth considering.

Boiler energy managers

There are many kinds of boiler energy managers available in the UK. Some are simple devices that delay a boiler firing, and work rather like just turning down the thermostat, whilst others are more complicated and are optimized for a particular model of boiler. Generally, simple strap-on devices are probably not a good investment, but if a boiler manufacturer recommends one for use with their specific model, then they are worth fitting at the time that the boiler is installed.

Full zone control

Most homes have a single heating zone control with TRV's controlling individual room temperatures. However, the need for heating in the main living rooms can be quite different from that in bedrooms where lower temperatures are required for longer hours. If a new central heating system is being installed, it is possible to fit a full zone control that has different pipe loops and separate thermostats for more than one area. This can save significant amounts of fuel, especially in larger houses.

Savings summary

table 4.2 financial and environmental savings (keeping warm – low cost actions)

Action	Cost (£)	Annual financial savings (£)	Payback (yrs)	Lifespan of product (yrs)	Lifetime savings for action (£)	Annual CO_2 savings (kg)	Lifetime CO_2 savings for action (tonnes)	£ spent/ tonne CO_2 saved
Fit radiator foil/panels	6[1]	15[2]	0.4	10+	150+	105	>1.0	<6
Draft proofing (DIY)	90[3]	18	5.0	20[3]	359	150[3]	3.0	30
Draft proofing (contractor)	200[3]	18	11.2	20[3]	359	150[3]	3.0	68
Heating controls upgrade[4]	200[3]	63	3.2	12[3]	760	530[3]	6.3	32

- Based on a three-bed semi-detached home.
- Assume 0.21 $kgCO_2$/kWh for gas consumption at a cost of 2.51p/kWh. If you have an electric-based heating system, the environmental and cost savings would be two–three times greater.
- Lifespan of products will vary depending on their quality, location and how well fitted.
- [1] Source: B&Q
- [2] Various sources.
- [3] Source: Energy Saving Trust.
- [4] Heating control costs assume the additional cost for installation when an installer is at the premises already working on the heating system.

Investment actions

Stop heat loss through insulation (general)

A quarter of the UK's carbon footprint is generated by our homes, and as we have seen above, largely due to heating them. Therefore insulating your home to reduce the rate at which heat escapes through the roof, walls, floors, windows and doors will make a large impact on your carbon footprint. Figure 4.4 illustrates the percentage heat losses from different parts of a house. Not only does insulation keep homes warm in the winter but it can also help to keep your house cool in summer. Many people are put off insulating their homes as they feel the inconvenience is too great. However, with a bit of time and energy, you can significantly reduce your heating bill and do your bit for the environment.

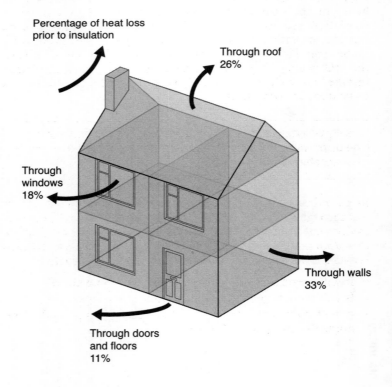

Percentage of heat loss prior to insulation

Through roof 26%

Through windows 18%

Through walls 33%

Through doors and floors 11%

figure 4.4 key areas of heat loss from an uninsulated house

Your local Energy Saving Trust Advice Centre is a good
for:

- free, impartial advice on home insulation and general
  savings tips
- advice on whether you are entitled to a grant or offer t
  pay for installation
- finding Energy-Saving Recommended insulation products.
  See **www.energysavingtrust.org.uk** or call 0800 512 012
  (free).

Cavity wall insulation

In most houses built after the 1920s, the outer walls consist of
two layers of bricks, with a gap (or 'cavity') between them (see
Figure 4.5). Initially the main purpose of cavity walls was to
help prevent damp penetrating the inner wall. But in 1955
legislation required all new built homes and extensions to
include insulation within the cavity wall to create warmer
homes (see Figure 4.6). Many houses, therefore built between
the 1920s and 1955 will not have had cavity wall insulation
installed due to its then relatively very high price, and so this has
to be done retrospectively.

> Cavity wall insulation fills the gap between the two layers of bricks
> on outer walls, acting like a 'thermos' flask to keep the air in your
> home naturally warm (or cool).

In an uninsulated home, approximately 33 per cent of heat is
lost through walls. This is more than any other route. Therefore,
cavity wall insulation is a fantastic way to significantly reduce
the amount of energy you need to heat your home, thereby
reducing your energy bills. It also has additional benefits:

- It will create a more even temperature in your home.
- It will reduce condensation on walls and ceilings.
- It will reduce the amount of heat building up inside your
  home during summer hot spells.

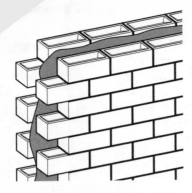

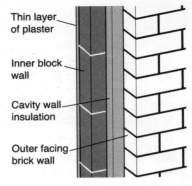

Thin layer of plaster

Inner block wall

Cavity wall insulation

Outer facing brick wall

figure 4.5 cavity wall with added foam insulation (older property)

figure 4.6 cavity wall with integral insulation (modern property)

According to the Energy Saving Trust, between 2002 and 2005 around 800,000 households installed cavity wall insulation. It is estimated that this will have saved nearly 400,000 tonnes of CO_2, enough to fill the new Wembley stadium 47 times.

Practicalities (cavity wall insulation):
- Cavity wall insulation is quick, clean and relatively inexpensive to install.
- In new-build properties or extensions, the easiest and quickest way to fit cavity wall insulation is using 75mm thick preformed slabs which fit snugly into the cavity. As well as insulating your home, these slabs are also water-repellent, provide additional sound-proofing and act as a fire retardant.
- In existing properties, small holes are drilled in the outer wall and insulation is injected at high pressure which then expands to fill the gap as shown in Figure 4.7. It only takes two to three hours to insulate a three-bedroom semi-detached house.
- Find a registered installer by visiting the Cavity Insulation Guarantee Agency (CIGA) (**http://www.ciga.co.uk/**) or the National Insulation Association (NIA) (**www.national-insulationassociation.org.uk**). CIGA provide a 25-year guarantee backed by millions of pounds of insurance!
- A cavity wall insulation service is available from B&Q.

figure 4.7 insulation being injected into cavity wall

If all the houses which currently have unfilled cavity walls had them filled, the energy saved could heat a staggering 1.4 million homes each year. (Source: Energy Saving Trust.)

Solid wall insulation

Many older houses (usually pre 1920s) do not have cavity walls, but single solid walls, which lose more heat than cavity walls. You should be able to identify if your house has a solid wall by the brick formation. In cavity walls, the bricks are evenly laid end to end, whereas in solid walls whole bricks alternate with half-bricks (see Figure 4.8).

figure 4.8 typical brick formation for solid walls

There are two methods of insulating solid walls:

- Internally – applied to the **inside** of the property.
- Externally – applied to the **outside** of the property.

As with cavity wall insulation there are similar additional benefits resulting from solid wall insulation, such as creating a more even temperature in your home. However, solid wall insulation is more expensive than cavity wall insulation, particularly external types.

You can find out more information on solid wall insulation from the National Insulation Association (NIA) (**www.nationalinsulationassociation.org.uk**).

Practicalities (internal wall insulation):

- Internal insulation is usually applied by 'dry-lining' with insulation material plus plasterboard, or a laminate of insulating plasterboard (conventional plasterboard with an integral backing of expanded polystyrene).
- A key factor when considering internal insulation is the amount of available space. Insulation/plaster board laminates can have a total thickness of up to 90mm and will, therefore,

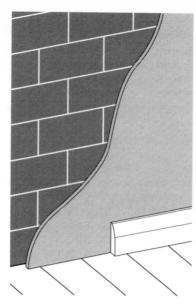

figure 4.9 internal insulation

reduce the size of a room. Materials which claim to have a higher thermal performance are available if space is at a premium.

- Fitting insulating plasterboard is not difficult. Once it has been cut to size it is simply glued and screwed into place after skirting boards and picture rails have been removed. Doors, windows, radiators, electric switches and sockets, may have to be repositioned or modified to account for the new 50–90mm layer of plasterboard.
- Alternatively you can attach wooden battens in-filled with insulation to a wall. These are then covered with plasterboard to finish.
- You can plaster directly onto insulation which has cost and speed advantages. It also gives non-uniform surfaces which may be desirable in older properties.
- Flexible insulating lining (another form of 'dry lining') can also be used. It is bought in rolls like wallpaper and is less expensive and easier to fit.

Practicalities (external wall insulation):

- Generally it is more expensive than internal wall insulation.
- It is usually only installed where there are severe heating problems or the exterior of the building requires some form of additional repair work thereby providing the opportunity for adding insulation.
- A decorative weather-proof insulating treatment is applied to the outside of your wall.
- The thickness of the insulation needs to be between 50 and 100mm.
- If a proprietary system is used the work must be carried out by a specialist contractor but local architect-designed systems can be installed by good general builders.
- Sometimes the roof details at eaves and verges need to be altered to fit and this can change the appearance of the building significantly.
- You can find out more information on external wall insulation from:
  - Insulated Render & Cladding Association (INCA) (**www.inca-ltd.org.uk**)
  - External Wall Insulation Association (EWIA) (**http://dubois.vital.co.uk/database/ceed/draught.html**) – maintains a register of proven systems and installers.

Loft insulation

Heat rises and much of it can be lost through the roof of your home, accounting for over a quarter of your heating bills if your roof is poorly insulated. Loft insulation is one of the easiest and most effective single improvements that you can make to your home to reduce energy use. It acts like a blanket, trapping heat rising from within the house. Many people consider boarding their lofts, using the space either for storage or extra living space. In these situations a different approach is required to effectively provide insulation.

If everyone insulated their lofts to the recommended level, it would save 4 million tonnes of CO_2 a year – enough to fill the new Wembley stadium 500 times over!

(Source: B&Q.)

Practicalities (loft insulation – general):

- You can carry out loft insulation yourself as a DIY task or you can employ a professional installer. There are usually grants and offers available to help you pay for it.

- If you plan to do it yourself, you need to protect yourself sufficiently with a facemask, goggles, gloves and protective clothing.

- Check first whether you already have any loft insulation and if so how much. To be effective, standard loft insulation needs to be at least 270mm (10 inches) thick. More than one type of insulation can be used and new insulation can be added to existing insulation.

- If your loft insulation is quite old, or if it is compressed under boarding, it may well be less effective. However, both these problems are relatively easy to fix.

- There are three main ways to insulate your loft:

  - **Blanket insulation** – Roll-out blanket type insulation between and over the joists. This is the most economical way to insulate your loft.

  - **Boarded lofts** – If your loft space is already boarded over then board type insulation provides a suitable surface for storing boxes.

  - Insulation for the rafters to convert the loft into a warm, usable room (**warm room lofts**).

- Don't forget to insulate the loft hatch!

- There is now a great choice of insulation materials available. Some, such as recycled paper and sheep's wool, are more environmentally friendly (lower embodied energy) than the usual mineral wool, but they can be a lot more expensive.

DIY

Some DIY stores are making it easier to plan and buy your loft insulation by stocking affordable and easy to install products with instructions that are simple to understand. One DIY store, B&Q, also provide an on line calculator (see **www.diy.com**) to help you work out more accurately how much product you need.

Practicalities (blanket loft insulation):

- In a new home or one where this is no insulation already, a roll-out product is ideal. It is ready perforated to fit the standard gaps between joists (usually 400mm or 600mm) and is easy to divide and fit by hand. If your loft space is not used for storage then lay insulation between and over the joists to 270mm thickness. This is the quickest and easiest solution and most lofts can be completed in around an hour.

- Start to lay blanket insulation at one side of the loft and unroll the material towards the middle. Tuck the end of the roll down into the eaves but don't completely block them as some ventilation is needed to prevent condensation.

- To prevent freezing, do not insulate under the cold water tank.

- When you reach the middle of the loft, cut the insulation. Go to the other end of the loft and start again, butting up the meeting edges in the middle. Repeat for each joist space ensuring that the blanket insulation is tucked under any electric wiring to avoid the risk of overheating.

- Next cross-lay a second layer of insulation above the joists. This needs to be laid at right angles to the first layer to avoid 'cold bridging' through gaps in the insulation blanket.

- Products are available in different thicknesses specifically for topping up existing loft insulation. Simply lay over your existing insulation to bring it up to an effective thickness. They are often encapsulated making them virtually itch-free so they are clean and easy to lay.

- Take extra care that corners are properly insulated as this is often where heat leaks are found.

- Once laid, be careful to stand only on the joists which will be under the second layer of insulation. Walk boards can be laid over the joists to provide safe access from the loft hatch to any water tanks (if present).

- When insulating over down-lighters, use a Down Light Heat Diffuser. This will ensure the insulation goes around rather than over the down lights and stops them from overheating.

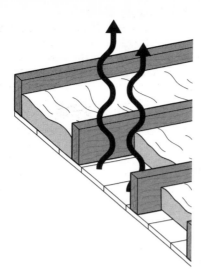

figure 4.10 blanket loft insulation

If everyone in the UK topped up their loft insulation to 270mm, £380million would be saved. That's enough money to pay the annual fuel bills of over 400,000 families. (Source: Energy Saving Trust.)

Practicalities (board loft insulation):

- Remove all stored goods and coverings from the loft boards then vacuum and clean thoroughly.
- Lay one layer of loft board insulation onto the boarded area only. Use a solvent-free adhesive to secure and ensure the loft board insulation is tightly butted. A sharp knife is needed to cut boards to fit.
- For maximum savings, a second layer of loft board insulation can be fixed over the first, again using a solvent-free adhesive. If you intend to walk on the floor, lay new chipboard over the insulation board.

Practicalities (warm room loft insulation):

- If you're converting your loft into living space, the insulation needs to be installed at rafter level.
- Insulation should be fitted between the rafters to a thickness of 170mm and then a vapour membrane and plasterboard placed over the top.
- Alternatively, if you are not converting your loft but simply wish to make it warmer you can use a variety of products to fit between rafters or top up insulation by stapling directly onto rafters.

Floor insulation and draught proofing

Practicalities (floor insulation):

- You can do many of the smaller jobs yourself with materials from your local DIY store and this may work out cheaper.
- Gaps and draughts around skirting boards and floorboards are simple to fix yourself with silicon sealant or with wooden beading. Beading should be pinned to the skirting rather than the floor so that the floor is allowed to move.
- A good quality carpet combined with thick underlay, or an insulating floor covering such as cork or cushion vinyl laid on hardboard, can minimize heat loss through the floor.
- Timber floors can be insulated by laying mineral wool insulation under the floorboards between the joists.
- You must ensure that under-floor airbricks in your outside walls are not blocked. Floorboards will rot without adequate ventilation.
- Under-floor insulation is worth considering if the floor is being excavated for other reasons or when a new floor is being laid. Otherwise it is an expensive option.

Savings summary (insulation)

table 4.3 financial and environmental savings (home insulation)

Action	Cost (£)	Annual financial savings (£)	Payback (yrs)	Lifespan of insulation (yrs)	Lifetime savings for action (£)	Annual CO_2 savings (tonnes)	Lifetime CO_2 savings for action (tonnes)	£ spent/ tonne CO_2 saved
Cavity wall insulation[1]	250[1]	91	2.8	40[2]	3,634	0.76[2]	30	8
Internal wall insulation	1,500[3] (£42/m²)	311	4.8	30[2]	9,323	2.6[2]	77	20
External wall insulation (during wall repair)[4]	1,900[2]	311	6.1	30[2]	9,323	2.6[2]	77	25
Adding 270mm loft insulation (no insulation to start with) – DIY	180[2]	114	1.6	40[2]	4,542	0.95[2]	37	5
Adding 270mm loft insulation (no insulation to start with) – Installer	500[2]	114	4.4	40[2]	4,542	0.95[2]	37	13
Adding loft insulation (topping up to 270mm from 50mm) – DIY	250[2]	32	7.7	40[2]	1,291	0.27[2]	11	24

(continues overleaf)

Action	Cost (£)	Annual financial savings (£)	Payback (yrs)	Lifespan of insulation (yrs)	Lifetime savings for action (£)	Annual CO_2 savings (tonnes)	Lifetime CO_2 savings for action (tonnes)	£ spent/ tonne CO_2 saved
Adding loft insulation (topping up to 270mm from 50mm) – Installer	500[2]	32	15.5	40[2]	1,291	0.27[2]	11	47
Floor insulation (DIY and only insulation)	90[2]	44	2.0	30[2]	1,327	0.37[2]	11	8
Filling gaps between floor and skirting board (DIY)	20[2]	16	1.3	15[2]	233	0.13[2]	2	10

Notes:
- Based on a typical three-bed semi-detached home. Cost savings vary with other property sizes and age – in general new flats and terrace properties use the least energy and so have the lowest potential savings from insulation. Large old properties have the most to gain.
- These figures are based on a gas heating system. Assume $0.21kgCO_2/kWh$ for gas consumption at a cost of 2.51p/kWh. If you have an electric-based heating system, the environmental and cost savings would be two–three times greater.
- [1]Installed costs assume that installation is undertaken by a professional installer and are subject to a discount from an energy supplier – for instance, with cavity wall insulation, British Gas offered (until July 07) a price of £225 for a three-bed house – even lower than price quoted in the table – otherwise according to the Energy Saving Trust, costs would be about £500.
- [2]Source: Energy Saving Trust.
- [3]This is a very approximate estimate because it depends on wall area coverage and how much you can do yourself. Energy Saving Trust quotes £42/m[2].
- [4]Installed costs assume that walls are being repaired anyway and only relates to the additional cost of insulation and labour.

Improved glazing of windows and doors

Approximately 20 per cent of the heat lost from an uninsulated home is lost through the windows (Source: Energy Saving Trust). Double glazing creates an insulating barrier by trapping air between two panes of glass and can reduce heat loss by half. This can be improved further with glazing systems that include special low-emmissivity glass and certain inert gases.

Other benefits of double glazing are:

- reduction of condensation
- reduction of external noise
- reduction of heat transmission in the summer.

Practicalities (improved glazing):

- Consider draught proofing first as a less expensive measure if you are on a tight budget.
- Look for the 'Energy Saving Recommended' logo when choosing your windows. The whole window, frame and glass, is assessed on a rating of A–G by the British Fenestration Ratings Council and so you can be sure they are the most energy efficient.

Rating windows

The British Fenestration Ratings Council (BFRC) (**www.bfrc.org**) coordinates the BFRC Window Energy Rating System, which helps you or your builder to quickly and reliably select energy efficient windows for your home by comparing window ratings. This site provides details of how to get windows energy rated, which windows are energy rated and which companies supply rated windows.

The basic label, as shown in Figure 4.11, gives details about the manufacturer, the product, essential energy performance data and also provides a source for additional information. It will give:

- **Thermal transmittance** (U-value) – This measures how effectively a product prevents heat loss.
- **Solar factor** (g-value) – This measures how effectively a product blocks heat caused by sunlight.
- **Air leakage** (L50 value).

Each rating label is specific to a manufacturer and is non-transferable. The BFRC Certificate Number relates to the specific certificate and details of the certificate can be obtained from their website.

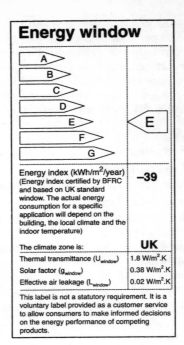

figure 4.11 energy label for windows (example)

- To find Energy Saving Recommended windows see Energy Saving Trust website (**www.energysavingtrust.org.uk**) or call 0800 512 012 (free).
- Request 'Low-e' glazing. The special heat-reflective coating reduces heat loss by nearly half (see below).
- Request **gas**-filled windows – they reduce heat loss further and can save even more money (see below).

What is a low emmissivity glass?

This is glass with a low emmissivity (low-e) coating which allows short wave radiation (light) to pass through but inhibits long wave radiation (heat). The coating is a very thin layer of metal or metal oxide on the glass which permits light to pass through from the outside to the inside of a building, but limits heat escaping from the inside to the outside of a building (see Figure 4.12).

Why add gas to windows?

Certain gases can be used to improve the performance of windows. Air between panes is replaced with more viscous, slow-moving gas, minimizing convection currents and, therefore, heat loss (see Figure 4.12). These gases are inert and non-toxic, and so do not pose any health or environmental risk if a window gets broken. The most commonly used gas is Argon, a gas found naturally in ordinary air.

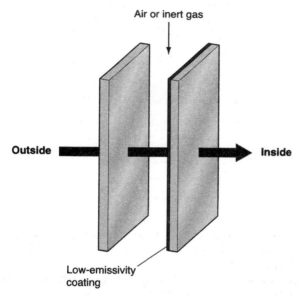

Air or inert gas

Outside　　　　　　　　　　　　　　**Inside**

Low-emissivity
coating

figure 4.12 high specification glazing

- Check the air gap between the panes – a 6mm or 8mm gap is not really enough, a 12mm to 20mm gap is more effective at stopping heat loss (as well as reducing noise.)
- You can place double glazing behind or in front of existing single-glazed units to further increase the level of insulation.
- Avoid UPVC frames – these are difficult to recycle and high in embodied energy costs. Good wooden framed glazing systems are available (see eco-merchants in the 'Taking it further' section).

- If you can't afford to replace all the windows, replace those in rooms that cost you the most to heat first.
- Less than airtight joinery is the most common weak point in any window. Fitting flexible joints (metal or rubber) on the edges of the window can reduce your heating costs by 15 per cent.
- Make sure that you still allow good ventilation.

table 4.4 financial and environmental savings (glazing)

Action	Cost (£)	Annual financial savings (£)	Payback (yrs)	Lifespan of glazing (yrs)	Lifetime savings (£)	Annual CO$_2$ savings (kg)	Lifetime CO$_2$ savings for action (tonnes)	£ spent/ tonne CO$_2$ saved
Installing double glazing	3,000	76	39	25	1,912	640	16	191

Notes:

- For any new build or extensions, you will have to install double glazing as a minimum as part of the current UK Building Regulations.
- Figures for installations costs, lifespan and CO$_2$ savings are from various sources.
- Based on a three-bed semi-detached home.
- These figures are based on a gas heating system. Assume 0.21kgCO$_2$/kWh for gas consumption at a cost of 2.51p/kWh. If you have an electric-based heating system, the environmental and cost savings would be two–three times greater.

Upgrade your boiler

Nearly 75 per cent of your household's CO_2 emissions come from your boiler, providing you with heating and water. This means that upgrading your boiler can have a large impact on your energy use. Since the lifespan of a boiler is about 15 years, and many of those currently installed will be 5–10 years old, most households will have an opportunity over the next few years to upgrade to newer, much more efficient models such as condensing boilers which were not available in the past.

What is a high efficiency condensing boiler?

A high efficiency condensing boiler recovers as much waste heat as possible, whereas a conventional (non-condensing) boiler normally loses this heat to the atmosphere via the flue. The best condensing boilers convert more than 90 per cent of their fuel into heat, compared to 60–78 per cent for conventional types.

Figure 4.13 illustrates how this is achieved by using a larger heat exchanger or sometimes two heat exchangers within the boiler. When in condensing mode the flue gases give up their 'latent heat' which is then recovered by the heat exchanger within the boiler. At the same time some water is produced. As a result the temperature of the gases exiting the flue of a condensing boiler is typically 50–60°C compared with 120–180°C in a current non-condensing boiler. (Source: Energy Saving Trust.)

Practicalities (boiler upgrade):

- If your boiler is more than 10–15 years old then it probably won't be efficient.
- To minimise cost and disruption, consider fitting a new high efficiency condensing boiler at the same time you're fitting a new kitchen or bathroom.
- By law, all new gas boilers now fitted in the UK, with a few exceptions, must be high efficiency condensing ones.
- There may be grants and offers available to help you install an energy efficient heating system.
- Ask your installer for an Energy Saving Recommended boiler and look for the logo on heating controls. It guarantees that the boiler is the most energy efficient in its category.

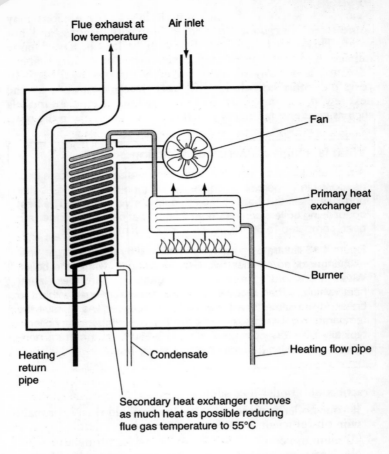

Flue exhaust at low temperature

Air inlet

Fan

Primary heat exchanger

Burner

Heating return pipe

Condensate

Heating flow pipe

Secondary heat exchanger removes as much heat as possible reducing flue gas temperature to 55°C

A fan draws heat from primary heat exchanger into secondary one, where cooler returning water reduces further the temperature of the hot flue gases.

figure 4.13 gas fired condensing boiler

Rating your boiler

When choosing a new boiler, check the energy rating. Like most new appliances, boilers carry a label rating them from A to G according to their energy efficiency. A is the most efficient (converting over 90 per cent of energy into heat). G is the least (below 70 per cent).

You can use a database to check the efficiencies of current and past domestic-sized boilers – Seasonal Efficiency of Domestic Boilers in the UK (SEDBUK) (**www.sedbuk.com**). There can be a difference of over 15 per cent in the efficiency of new boilers.

- Make sure your installer is CORGI registered; they should be able to fit a condensing boiler. In the past builders were hesitant about installing condensing boilers because there were only a limited number of models available and they were more expensive than other boiler types. See CORGI website: **http://www.trustcorgi.com/consumers.htmx** or call 0870 401 2300.

- Prices have fallen significantly over recent years, so there are fewer grants or offers available. However, it is still worth checking for offers – try your gas provider, local council, local Energy Efficiency Advice Centre or contact the Energy Savings Trust – call 0800 512 012 or see **ww.energysaving-trust.org.uk**).

- Most new and indeed old heating systems are compatible with high efficiency condensing boilers. Ask your installer for more details.

- For oil-fired systems seek professional advice from an OFTEC registered installer (**www.oftec.co.uk** or call 0845 6002105).

Sizing up your new boiler!

Replacement boilers are rarely sized correctly. Oversized boilers cost more to purchase and generally operate less efficiently resulting in higher running costs and increased emissions to the atmosphere. If additional insulation (such as loft or cavity wall insulation) has been installed since the last boiler was fitted in a particular house, it is highly likely that you can downsize to a smaller boiler than before. Most existing boilers are measured by their output in British Thermal Units per hour (Btu/h), and current boilers are sold in the metric equivalent of kilowatts (kW). Seek professional advice from a CORGI (gas-fired) or OFTEC (oil-fired) registered installer before choosing a replacement boiler. Alternatively, there are online resources to help you or your installer to more accurately assess the optimal size – see the Boiler Efficiency Database at **www.boilers.org.uk** or **www.sedbuk.com**.

Can condensing boilers work with warm air systems?

In general, condensing boilers can be used with warm air central heating. Since these systems were commonly fitted into homes in the late 1960s and 1970s, many are now in need of a major upgrade or replacement. There are a limited number of UK firms specializing in this work, including *Johnson & Starley* who maintain a library with the technical specifications of almost all warm air system types ever installed in the UK. New or upgraded warm air systems must comply with the British Standard BS 5864:2004. This applies to warm air heaters that incorporate a fan, to combined air heater/circulator installations and to heaters that distribute warm air by natural convection.

If everyone in the UK who could, installed a condensing boiler, CO_2 emissions would be cut by 13 million tonnes and the energy saved would heat every household in Scotland and Wales for a year! (Source: Energy Saving Trust.)

Combi (combination) boilers

Combi boilers work by heating water directly from the cold mains as and when you need it. This means you do not need a water tank or exposed pipes in your loft. It also means your water comes through at mains pressure, so you do not need an extra pump to boost your shower.

table 4.5: financial and environmental savings (upgrade of boiler)

Action	Cost (£)	Annual financial savings (£)	Payback (yrs)	Lifespan of boiler (yrs)	Lifetime savings for appliance (£)	Annual CO_2 savings (kg)	Lifetime CO_2 savings for action (tonnes)	£ spent/ tonne CO_2 saved
Upgrade to a high efficiency condensing boiler	400[1]	90	4.5	12[2]	1,076	750[2]	9	45

Notes:

- By law, all new gas boilers now fitted in the UK, with a few exceptions, must be high efficiency condensing ones. Therefore if you are forced to replace your boiler, the payback is less relevant.

- Based on a three-bed semi-detached home. Cost savings vary with other property type. In general, new flats and terrace properties use the least energy and so have the lowest potential savings and large old detached properties have the most to gain.

- These figures are based on a gas heating system. Assume $0.21kgCO_2/kWh$ for gas consumption at a cost of 2.51p/kWh.

- [1]Purchase cost based on average B&Q price, August 2007 (£300–£500). Does not include cost of installation.

- [2]Source: Energy Saving Trust.

Use sunspaces/conservatories to heat homes

A **sunspace** is a glass covered area attached to a dwelling that is heated primarily by solar gain (sunshine), but also by the heat losses from the building. The glazing allows the light to enter the sunspace, which is then converted to heat when it is absorbed by any surface and is then retained by the insulative properties of the glazing. Figure 4.14 indicates how a shallow winter sun can penetrate deeper into a building providing more light and potential heat gains to the main building. The more intense summer sun at a higher angle can have its heat impact reduced by allowing the main building to self-shade itself. A **conservatory** is a form of sunspace that provides additional amenity value for house occupants in the form of a pleasant living space, but its main focus is not to save heating costs.

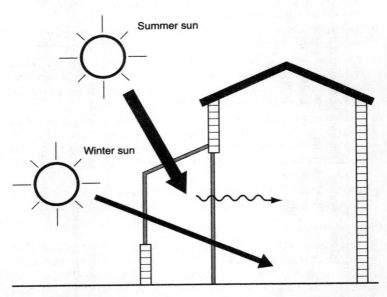

figure 4.14 use of glazed sunspace to heat a home (© Hockerton Housing Project)

The benefits:

- **Additional heat source** – A sunspace has the potential to reduce the overall heating requirements of the home by making the heat gained from it available to the main part of the house. When the temperature in the sunspace is greater than the main dwelling space, doors and windows can be opened to bring heat inside and reduce the need for dedicated heating. This reduction in space heating requirements has been suggested to range from 25 per cent in Scotland to 60 per cent in North America, the range being due to differences in direct solar radiation.

- **Added insulation** – A sunspace provides an additional insulation layer to the walls and windows of the main part of the dwelling. This is most useful in the winter, reducing heat loss from those parts of the building. This is referred to as buffering, or creating a buffer zone.

- **Draught lobby** – Sunspaces used as porches reduce heat loss by acting as an air-lock when external doors are opened.

- **Evening heat** – Heat is stored and radiated by the solid structures inside a sunspace such as the brickwork. In this way, sunspaces can continue to provide warmth long into the evening, as the external temperature cools down.

- **Hot water** – Sunspaces may also be used to preheat water as part of a hot water system. Solar thermal panels can be incorporated into the roof structure or, alternatively, heat gains can be made simply from the hot air to pipes or panels within the sunspace.

- **Drying facility** – Sunspaces offer an effective substitute for energy-hungry tumble dryers and outside washing lines.

The problem:

The problem is that many conservatories are poorly designed in terms of energy use, with conventional heating systems being added to make them comfortable. Few conservatories are insulated as well as the rest of the house, so much of the heat will escape through the glass. The result is that rather than taking advantage of solar gain to reduce heating for the dwelling overall, more heating is used to make this additional space available at a comfortable temperature. Therefore, they usually end up as a net liability in energy terms!

How to improve use of sunspaces:

The effectiveness and energy efficiency of the sunspace can be improved by doing the following:

- **Not adding space heating!**
- A wide but shallow depth sunspace will outperform a narrow but deep conservatory in the crucial winter period.
- A south-east aspect is preferable in the UK as the conservatory benefits throughout the day from the early morning sun. Overheating is reduced as it will be shaded from westerly sun at times when the outside temperature is at its highest.
- More advanced glazing (e.g. double glazing using low-e glass) will reduce overheating in the summer and reduce heat losses at all times.
- Increasing the amount of thermal mass of the building, such as brickwork or floor tiles, where heat energy from the sun is absorbed, stored and then gradually released. The greater the mass the more heat can be stored and the more even temperature will ensure that the temperature remains in the comfort zone for longer.
- A solid insulated roof will improve performance throughout the year by reducing heat loss in winter and overheating in summer. This still allows for useful gains in the winter from a shallow sun being able to enter through horizontal glazing but shades the space from overheating in the summer.
- Good high level ventilation will reduce overheating.

Build a porch

Building a **porch** can help to reduce heat loss from your home by creating a buffer zone from the cold, especially if your external doors open directly from the outside to a heated indoor space, such as a lounge. It will also cut down on draughts.

A few additional points:

- Porches that face south and have large windows and solid floors such as quarry tiles can warm the air as well, a bit like a sunspace (see previous section). However, if this is the case, fit an opening window in case it gets too hot.
- Make sure the exterior door is of exterior quality to keep out draughts and keep your home secure. It is possible to purchase well-insulated doors that include double or even triple glazing.

- A glazed porch should not be heated as it will waste more energy than it saves. If you want to build a heated porch, make sure that the windows take up no more than half the wall area. The remaining wall area should be constructed with properly insulated cavity walls.
- Make sure the porch doesn't cover a boiler flue.
- Make the porch big enough so that you can close one door before the other door is opened, in essence creating a temperature 'air-lock'. Also, on a practical note, make it wide enough to deal with bags of shopping or change of shoes.
- If there's no space outside for a porch, see if there's enough space inside to build a **draught lobby** with an inner door.

Hot water

No cost actions

- Check that your water thermostat is not set at too high a temperature. Ideally, it should be set to 60°C (140°F) and not lower than 55°C to reduce risk of legionnaire's disease.
- Only heat your water when you need it. A full tank of hot water, however well insulated, will always lose heat and need topping up by the boiler. Set your programmer to heat up your tank 30–45 minutes before you most commonly need a supply of hot water during the day.
- Ensure taps are turned off fully and fix any that leak – a dripping hot water tap wastes energy and over time can quickly add up (to prove this, put a plug in the bath or sink and see how quickly it fills up!).
- Take a shower rather than a bath – a five-minute shower consumes approximately half the amount of water, and energy, that a full bath takes. If you add a fine spray attachment to your shower you will use even less water. Beware of power showers as they may use as much as a bath, if not more. If you do have a bath, you could save energy by encouraging more than one member of the household to use the water!
- You could go one step further to reducing water and energy for personal hygiene – have a stand-up wash instead of a bath or a shower. This is particularly suitable in warm weather or in a well-heated bathroom.

sulate under the bath to keep your bath water warm for longer, avoiding the need for hot water top-ups.

- Insulate the hot water or immersion tank – you can buy a jacket for your hot water cylinder from your local DIY store. **This is one of the simplest and cheapest things you can do to cut your fuel bills and save energy.** Otherwise you could be losing up to 75 per cent of the energy you are buying to heat your hot water.

- Standing heat losses from the hot water dead leg (amount of water required to be run through pipes before reaching desired temperature by user) can be considerable. This can be reduced by insulating the hot water pipes. Fitting insulation to pipes is easy if the pipes are accessible but you may need professional help for harder to reach pipework (see Figure 4.15).

- Install a low-flow showerhead to reduce the amount of hot water used per shower.

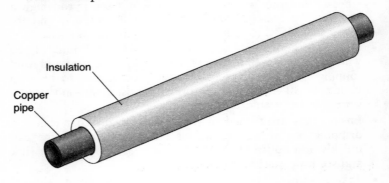

figure 4.15 pipe insulation

Practicalities (insulating hot water tanks):

- Fitting a jacket to a hot water cylinder is a relatively straight forward DIY job. Make sure the jacket is at least 80mm thick (see Figure 4.16).

- You can, however, go much further than 80mm insulation if you are willing to practise those DIY skills and you have the space. You may have to use a mix of rigid and other forms of insulation in combination with a frame. My tank has a minimum of 250mm of insulation, including under the base and on top, the result is hot water for about 30p a day!

- Most new cylinders now come pre-insulated with foam sprayed on them. However, don't let this stop you adding further insulation!

- It is also worth insulating the pipes that enter and leave the cylinder (see Figure 4.15) – you can buy foam tubes for doing just this. Do it as far back from the cylinder as you can reach.

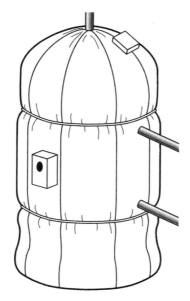

figure 4.16 hot water cylinder with insulating jacket

Investment actions

Upgrade your water heater

If your water heater is more than ten years old it is likely to be running at less than 50 per cent efficiency. Upgrading to a new, more efficient model will not only reduce your costs, but your environmental impact. (See 'Keeping warm' earlier in this chapter, for more info about upgrading boilers.)

Savings summary

table 4.6 financial and environmental savings (hot water)

Action	Cost (£)	Annual financial savings (£)	Payback (yrs)	Lifespan of action (yrs)	Lifetime savings for action (£)	Annual CO₂ savings (kg)	Lifetime CO₂ savings for action (tonnes)	£ spent/ tonne CO₂ saved
New hot water cylinder jacket (80mm) – DIY	12[1]	18	0.7	15	269	150[2]	2	5
Insulation for hot water pipes – DIY	4[1] (58p per metre)	8	0.5	20	155	65[2]	1	3
Turn off or fix dripping taps	n/a	2	n/a	n/a	n/a	20[3]	n/a	n/a
Install a low-flow showerhead	15	27	0.5	10	275	230[3]	2	7

Notes:

- Assume $0.21 kgCO_2/kWh$ for gas consumption at a cost of 2.51p/kWh. If you have an electric-based hot water system, the environmental and cost savings would be two–three times greater.

- [1]Purchase costs based on B&Q prices, August 2007.

- [2]CO_2 emissions – Source: Energy Saving Trust.

- [3]CO_2 emissions – Source: www.mycarbonfootprint.eu (calculator produced by European Commission – the calculator clearly defines the assumptions for figure used).

Tankless water heaters

Heating a large tank of water to a set temperature is the most common and best suited system for larger households that use a lot of hot water. Although such systems have become more efficient over the years, energy is still wasted when the hot water is not being used (standby energy loss).

An alternative is a system that uses 'tankless' water heaters, also known as 'on-demand' or 'instantaneous' heaters. These devices use energy only when hot water is needed, resulting in less standby energy loss. Although they tend to have a higher up-front cost, they are less expensive to operate in the long term due to their higher efficiency. When choosing a tankless water heater, you will have to calculate your required flow rate, or the total hot water consumption of the appliances you need to run simultaneously.

In the kitchen and utility area

No cost actions

General

- Avoid leaving appliances on standby and/or on charge unnecessarily (see 'Standby' later in this chapter).
- It is most efficient to wait until you can use full loads for the washing machine, tumble dryer or dishwasher. However, if you can't wait until you have a full load, then use the half-load or economy programme.
- Share appliances and equipment with neighbours and friends – how often do you really use that carpet cleaner? Save money and save the energy associated with more appliances having to be manufactured than really needed.

Fridges/Freezers

Although fridges and freezers may not seem to use much energy at any one moment, the fact that they have to be left on continually means that they make up a significant proportion of electricity use in many homes.

Easy to do:

- Minimize the time fridge and freezer doors/lids are open. It helps if you decide what you want before opening.

- Check guidelines from the manufacturer to ensure your fridge and freezer are set to the correct temperature. You could be using up to 25 per cent more energy than you need if the temperature is set below requirements. Generally, fridges don't need to be cooler than 3°C. You could put a thermometer in your fridge to monitor the temperature.
- Let hot food cool down before putting it into the fridge (or freezer).
- Cover liquids and wrap foods stored in the fridge. Uncovered foods release moisture and force the fridge to work harder.

Small effort:

- Defrost food from the freezer by putting it in the fridge the night before you want to use it. This will this help keep your fridge cold, and reduce its power consumption.
- Keep your fridge and freezer full (but not so full that air can't circulate) – it takes less energy to cool a full appliance than an empty one. The mass of cold items inside the appliance will also help it recover each time the door is opened. If you don't have enough food to fill it, you could use plastic bottles filled with water.
- Make sure fridges and freezers are not rammed up against a wall so that there is enough space for air to circulate and allow the appliance to operate more efficiently.
- Store fruit and vegetables in a cold pantry/larder, rather than the fridge – this reduces how often you have to open and close the fridge, and it may reduce the temptation for a second or larger fridge.

More effort:

- Regularly defrost manual-defrost refrigerators and freezers; frost buildup increases the amount of energy needed to keep the motor running. Don't allow frost to build up more than 5mm thick.
- Check door seals regularly to ensure they're airtight. To test them, close the door on a piece of paper and try to pull it out. If it slides out easily, you're wasting energy and money.
- Avoid placing your fridge or freezer in a warm spot. Locating fridges or freezers next to ovens, boilers or in direct sunlight increases energy consumption.
- Clean and dust down the coils at the back of the fridge and freezer.

- Do you have a spare fridge in the garage to keep those beers cold? If you don't truly need it, pass it on to someone that could make better use of it.

Cooking

Easy to do:

- Put a lid on your kettle or pan when boiling water; it's faster, uses less energy, and reduces condensation problems.
- Using an electric kettle to pre-boil water for cooking is more energy efficient, but make sure you only boil what you need.
- When cooking on an electric hob, turn the ring down or off several minutes before the allotted cooking time. It takes less heat to keep a pot boiling than it does to bring it to the boil and, once the ring is turned off, the residual heat in the element will finish cooking the food for you. The same principle applies when cooking in the oven; you can use residual heat to finish the cooking process.
- Match the size of the pan to the heating element so that you don't waste energy by heating the surrounding air or pan handle!
- When boiling vegetables use just sufficient water to cover them.
- When using a conventional oven, use the top shelf to cook food more quickly – it will be hotter than the bottom.
- Reduce pre-heating time when using a conventional oven. Unless you're baking breads or pastries, it may not be necessary to pre-heat.
- Don't open the oven door too often when checking your food; every time you do the oven temperature drops significantly. Use the window, clock or timer instead.
- Close the oven door gently as slamming forces out some of the precious hot air.

Some effort:

- Use a toaster for bread rather than under a grill if possible.
- Chop vegetables into small pieces before cooking – they will cook more quickly.
- Use flat-bottomed pans on electric hobs that make full contact with the element. A misshapen or rounded pan will waste a lot of the heat.
- Plan ahead, for example:
  - Get ready-made meals out of the freezer early enough for them to defrost in the fridge or at room temperature, avoiding the use of extra energy.

- Try and get as many things in the oven at the same time.
- If you have choice, cook things in the oven rather than on the hob; it is more efficient because the heat stays in the oven.
- Steaming is a great way to save energy because you can cook several items at once on the same ring. Potatoes, pasta or rice are placed in the bottom pan with water whilst vegetables are placed in steamer pans above. The steam from the bottom rises and cooks the vegetables above.

More effort:
- Use a pressure cooker; as well as saving up to two-thirds of the energy, it will save you time and preserve the goodness of your food.
- Use a 'slow cooker' – the food gently simmers for several hours using little more power than a conventional light bulb.

Washing and drying clothes

Easy to do:
- Wash at lower temperatures. Even if labels suggest washing at higher temperatures, modern washing powders and detergents work just as effectively at lower temperatures of 30°C or 40°C; so unless you have very dirty washing, there is no need to use higher temperatures. Washing at 60°C uses almost twice as much energy as a 40°C wash.
- Limit ironing to necessities. Many clothes can be folded or hung carefully to avoid ironing, whilst with some clothes there is just no point (e.g. kids sports clothes). By planning your ironing sessions you can save energy if you start with the hottest setting and then work your way down to clothes that need a cooler setting. Finally, turn the iron off when you are near the bottom of the pile – the residual heat will be enough to iron the last items very well.

Think climate – wash at 30°C

A number of companies that provide clothing are now actively encouraging their customers to lower their washing temperature. For example, since July 2007, Marks & Spencer have been putting new 'Think climate – wash at 30°C' labels in those clothes which can effectively be washed at this lower temperature (see Figure 4.17), saving around 40 per cent energy per wash.

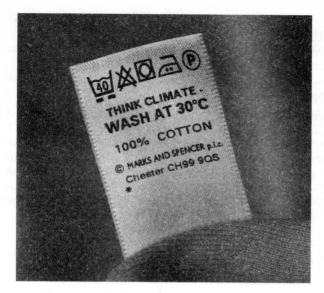

figure 4.17 M&S 'wash at 30°C' label

Some effort:

- Don't automatically toss anything that has been worn once or ended up on the floor into the laundry bin. Are they truly dirty? You could cut the number of loads you wash by airing clothes and putting them back in the cupboard if they're not really dirty.
- Use cool water when washing and rinsing by hand. Most non-greasy dirt will wash out easily with cold water and detergent.
- Wait until you've got a full load before using your washing machine if you can – using the 'half load' programme does not save you half the energy.
- If you use a tumble dryer, then spin dry or wring the clothes well before putting them in. This improves the efficiency and your clothes will dry more quickly.
- Soak very dirty laundry before washing; you could leave it to soak in your bath water after you have finished your bath.

More effort:

- If possible, connect both your hot and cold washing machine hoses to your hot and cold water pipes. This will enable the machine to use hot water from your tank rather than having

to heat cold water from scratch. (Note – many new appliances are only able to take a cold feed.)
- Avoid using tumble dryers – why not go back to hanging clothes outside whenever you can? (See Figure 4.18.)

Peg back your bills!

Families are returning to pegging out their washing to save money – and the planet. The supermarket ASDA has seen a 1,400 per cent increase in the sale of pegs in the first four months of 2007, compared with a year before. Sales of washing lines and rotary dryers are up by 147 per cent. The trend indicates a move away from tumble dryers which use huge amounts of energy, so contributing to the release of carbon and climate change. (Source: *Daily Mail* website, 13/06/07.)

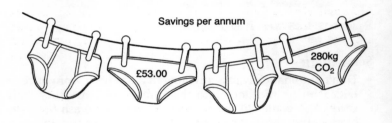

figure 4.18 hang out those savings! (© Hockerton Housing Project)

Dishwashers

Easy to do:

- Use 'economy' or 'eco' programmes (short wash cycles) if an option is provided, for everything except the dirtiest dishes. They use less energy and take less time.
- Switch your dishwasher off completely when it has finished, rather than continuing to use energy on standby.

Some effort:

- Wait until you have a full load before using your dishwasher. The 'half load' facility is not as energy efficient per item.

- Hand wash in the basin when you only have a few items.
- Avoid using the 'rinse hold' setting on your dishwasher. This uses more hot water for each use.
- Check the manufacturer's recommendations on water temperature; many models have internal heating elements that give you the option to set the water heater to a lower temperature. Experiment and see how low you can get and still have clean dishes.

More effort:
- When washing dishes by hand, fill the wash and rinse basins rather than letting the water run from the taps. This way you will use far less water than a dishwasher would.
- Locate your dishwasher away from your fridge and freezer, as its heat and moisture will increase your fridge's energy consumption. If you have to put them next to each other, you could place a sheet of foam insulation between them.

Kettles

Although electric kettles are only small electrical appliances, they consume more energy than you might think because they are used very frequently, often heat more water than is required, and have to bring the water up to boiling point – an extremely energy-intensive process.

Easy to do:
- Only boil as much water as you need (ensure that the electrical element is covered). Kettles that show you how much water is inside make this easier, particularly if they provide guidance on much you need per cup.

> If all Europeans boiled just the water they needed, thus avoiding 1 litre of unnecessarily boiled water per day, the energy saved could power one third of Europe's streetlights. (Source: **www.mycarbonfootprint.eu** – calculator produced by European Commission.)

Some effort:
- De-scale your kettle regularly to make it more efficient. Use a 2:1 mixture of water and vinegar and leave overnight. Rinse well, fill with clean water, boil and throw it away.

More effort:
- Make up a thermos flask of hot water, tea or coffee. This will save having to boil the kettle every time you need a drink.

Savings summary

table 4.7 financial and environmental savings (kitchen/utility – no cost actions)

Action	Annual cost savings (£)	Annual energy savings (kWh)	Annual CO_2 savings (kg)
Place fridge in a cool environment	28	283	150[1]
Let hot food cool down to room temperature before putting it in the fridge	1	11	6[2]
Only use the washing machine when it's full	8	85	45[3]
Dry clothes naturally instead of using a tumble dryer	53	528	280[4]
Boil just enough water for your hot drink	5	47	25[5]
Put your washing on at 40°C, not 60°C	10	98	52[6]

Notes:

- Assume $0.53 kgCO_2/kWh$ for electricity consumption at a cost of 10p/kWh.
- CO_2 emission savings – Source: **www.mycarbonfootprint.eu** – calculator produced by European Commission – Selected assumptions (for full details of assumptions see website).
- [1]This is based on the assumption that the fridge is moved from a place where the temperature is 30°C to one where the temperature is 20°C. This is also based on a new fridge/freezer that consumes 500kWh per year in a 30°C surrounding. If you have an older fridge you can avoid even higher CO_2 emissions.

- [2]The temperature of the fridge is assumed to be 4°C.
- [3]This is based on a standard European washing machine that is used for about 240 washing cycles a year. It is also assumed that half of these yearly washing cycles are half full. This implies that you can do the same total wash load by reducing the number of cycles to 75 per cent of today's total amount.
- [4]This is based on a standard European dryer that is used for about 150 drying cycles a year.
- [5]In this calculation it is assumed that 1 litre of boiled water is avoided per day and that the avoided water would have been heated from 10°C to 100°C.
- [6]Source: British Gas.

Low cost actions – upgrade appliances to more energy efficient ones

General tips for best savings

- Research properly before you buy. The 'Ethical Consumer' magazine and 'Which' are good sources of advice on the best buys.
- Within the EU, electrical goods such as fridges, freezers, laundry appliances, dishwashers and electric ovens, are required by law to carry an energy-efficient label (see Figure 4.19). They are labelled A–G with A being the highest rating. For fridges and freezers the EU energy label goes up to A++.
- Look for the 'Energy Saving Recommended' logo (see Figure 2.4) ('Energy Start' in US) when you purchase an appliance. This guarantees that the product is the most energy efficient in its category, i.e. it will cost less to run.

Fridges and freezers

Fridges and freezers are in many cases the hardest working appliances in the kitchen, being on constantly. Therefore it is worth checking to see how old they are as you can make real savings by using one of the latest energy efficient models.

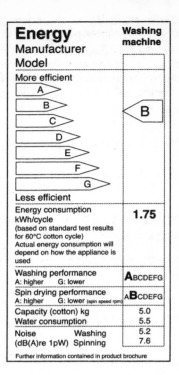

figure 4.19 example of an appliance energy label

Chilling thought!

UK households spend £1.6 billion every year on electricity to power their fridges and freezers. If everyone upgraded their fridges and freezers to Energy Saving Recommended ones, energy would be cut by two thirds, saving £900 million and the equivalent CO_2 emissions of 600,000 homes. (Source: Energy Saving Trust.)

Tips:

- Choose the most appropriate size fridge or freezer for your requirements, which may of course change over time.
- If you find your freezer is often half empty, rethink if you actually need one or, if you could replace it with a smaller model.

- Chest freezers are typically more efficient than upright freezers, because they're better insulated and cold air doesn't spill out when the door is opened.
- One large fridge is cheaper to run than two smaller ones so if you have a second fridge somewhere for all those 'extras' then consider getting rid of it and replacing with a single larger one.

Cooking

- Fan-assisted ovens run more efficiently than a conventional electric oven.
- Consider buying a self-cleaning oven. They use less energy for normal cooking because of higher insulation levels. They also save on your rubber glove and cleanser purchases! However, if you use the self-cleaning feature more than once a month, you'll end up using more energy than you saved. When you clean the oven, do it right after cooking to take advantage of residual heat (source: Tip the Planet, **www.tiptheplanet.com**).
- Halogen elements and induction elements are more efficient than conventional electric coil elements, but you must use the proper cookware. Induction elements require that you use only iron or steel pots and pans – aluminum cookware will not work.

Induction cooking

Usually a ferromagnetic coated pan is placed on an induction coil for the heating process to take place. This type of hob (stove top or cooktop in America) does not work with non-ferromagnetic cookware, such as glass, aluminum and most stainless steel, nor with ferromagnetic material covered with a conductive layer, such as a copper-bottomed pan.

Induction cookers are faster and more energy-efficient than traditional hobs. Also, the risk of accidental burning is reduced since the hob itself only gets marginally hot. No heat is lost to the air directly from the hob, keeping the kitchen cooler. Since heat is being generated from an electric current induced by an electric coil, the hob can detect when a pan is removed or its contents boil over by monitoring the resistance to the current. This allows a pan to be kept at minimal boil and the coil automatically turns off when the pan is removed. (Source: Wikipedia.)

Washing machines

- Select the most appropriate size to suit your average load size.
- The less water used by the machine on an average wash cycle, the less energy used to heat it. So choose a model that uses less water.
- Front loading machines use less water than top loaders. Although top loaders generally have faster washing times (typically 30–45 minutes), they use more water which means that on a warm wash they use more energy.
- Some washing machines have weight-sensitive functionality. They select the right amount of water for the weight of clothes in the load.

If everyone in the UK replaced their old washing machine with an Energy Saving Recommended model, over 440,000 tonnes of CO_2 could be saved, enough to fill more than 2.5 million double decker buses! (Source: Energy Saving Trust.)

Kettles

Electric kettles vary in the amount of electricity they consume. When you need to replace yours, choose one with the minimum energy consumption. For instance, the ECO Kettle has features that help to ensure you only boil the amount of water required, thus saving energy and carbon emissions (see Figure 4.20).

ECO kettle

It is estimated that, on average, we boil twice the volume of water needed every time. Which means twice as much energy and time. With a 3kW kettle that's the same as wasting the energy of around 50 light bulbs!

The ECO Kettle is different: its internal reservoir holds a full capacity of water ready for use, while the measuring button allows any quantity – from a single cupful to full capacity – to be released into the separate chamber for boiling.

The result? Exactly the right amount of water every time you boil – and no more waste. The ECO kettle has been awarded the 'Energy Saving Recommended' mark (see Figure 2.4) by the Energy Saving Trust (EST). This is first award to be given in the EST's newly established Kettle category, and endorses the 31 per cent average energy savings achieved by the ECO Kettle in independent trials. Based upon average usage figures, it is estimated that ECO Kettles sold over the past two years have already reduced CO_2 emissions in the UK by a staggering 500 tonnes! (Source **www.ecokettle.com**.)

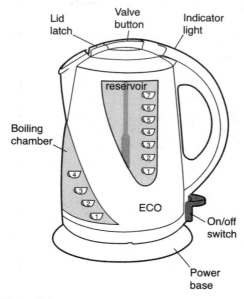

figure 4.20 the ECO kettle

Savings summary

Table 4.8 financial and environmental savings (kitchen/utility low cost actions)

Action	Cost (£)	Annual financial savings (£)	Payback (yrs)	Lifespan of appliance (yrs)	Lifetime savings for appliance (£)	Annual CO_2 savings (kg)	Lifetime CO_2 savings for action (tonnes)	£ spent/ tonne CO_2 saved
Fridge/freezer	From 218	28	7.8	13	363	148	1.9	115
Fridge/freezer (marginal)	50	28	1.8	13	363	148	1.9	26
Upright/chest freezer	From 200	21	9.7	13	267	109	1.4	143
Upright/chest freezer (marginal)	50	21	2.4	13	267	109	1.4	36
Fridge	From 150	12	12.4	13	157	64	0.8	183
Fridge (marginal)	20	12	1.7	13	157	64	0.8	24
Dishwasher	From 180	16	11.2	9	144	85	0.8	239
Washing machine	From 200	8	25.2	10	79	42	0.4	484
Washing machine (marginal)	50	8	6.3	10	79	42	0.4	121

Notes on upgrading appliances:

- Purchase costs based on John Lewis prices, August 2007.
- *Marginal costs* are the estimated additional costs of an A-rated appliance and it is assumed that the appliance is being changed anyway. In some cases the costs may be lower.
- Assume $0.53kgCO_2/kWh$ for electricity consumption at a cost of 10p/kWh
- CO_2 emission savings assume replacing an average appliance purchased new in 1995 with an Energy Saving Recommended model (A-rated dishwashers/washing machines, or A+/A++ refrigeration appliances) of similar size. Savings for A++ cold appliances are, on average, £6/yr greater (source: Energy Saving Trust).
- Lifespan – estimate based on variety of sources, including National Association of Home Builders (US).
- Washing machine run an average of 274 cycles a year. Energy Saving Recommended dishwashers and washing machines also use less water – if your water is metered, you'll also save money by using less water per wash cycle (source: Energy Saving Trust).

Computers, TVs and gadgets

Flat-screen televisions, computers and other hi-tech gadgets will use nearly half of a typical household's total electricity by 2020, according to 'The Ampere Strikes Back' report produced in 2007 by the Energy Saving Trust (EST). Here are some key points that the report makes:

- Consumer electronics will overtake kitchen appliances and lighting as the biggest single drain on domestic power.
- New devices are often more power-hungry than earlier models and many are left on standby rather than being switched off, leaving them in a permanent state of readiness to swing into action. Some don't even have an 'off' button.
- In 1982, only 3 per cent of homes had a personal computer compared to 60 per cent today. Similarly, printer ownership has shot up from 0.7 per cent to 58 per cent.
- Houses often have more than one TV and people are buying larger screens that use more energy.
- By 2020, TVs on standby will consume 1.4 per cent of all domestic electricity.

- Despite attempts by some manufacturers to make more energy-efficient products, some digital radios still use four times as much power as analogue sets.
- The growth of single person households, many with big TVs, set-top boxes, computers, games consoles, TV and music recorders and digital radios, will add to the higher energy consumption.
- Households could save £37 a year on their energy bill simply by switching devices off at the wall.

Other, less typical equipment, may contribute significantly to individual household electricity consumption where used, such as:

- hi-fi amplifiers
- home cinema equipment
- additional kitchen appliances such as food processors, blenders, coffee makers, etc.
- personal care equipment such as hair dryers, curlers, straighteners, etc.
- games consoles, etc.

Electronic pollution – a wider issue

Large amounts of energy and raw materials are needed to produce computers and other electronic equipment, and dealing with the electronic waste when these items are disposed of is a growing problem.

Televisions and other electronic goods are made of copper, lead and iron as well as plastic. Large amounts of energy are used in the extraction and processing of these materials. In addition, the manufacturing process results in harmful emissions into the atmosphere, contributing to climate change and air pollution.

It is estimated that the average UK citizen will generate a staggering 3.3 tonnes of electronic waste over their lifetime. This mountain of waste needs to be handled properly since the hazardous chemicals contained within the items can cause serious environmental pollution. A new EU law now means that manufacturers have to take back old, discarded electronic goods from customers or, alternatively, deliver them to an appropriate collection facility free of charge.

By cutting down on energy use, and disposing of unwanted equipment carefully, you can reduce the harmful impact of electronic goods on the environment.

Greenpeace (**www.greenpeace.org**) have produced a 'Green Electronics Guide' that ranks leading mobile and PC manufacturers on their global policies and practices on eliminating harmful chemicals. Companies are ranked out of ten and the guide is updated every three months.

No cost actions

Easy to do:

• Only charge your phone/PDA/iPod for as long as it needs – unplug the chargers when batteries are fully charged or when the chargers are not in use.

• When you have finished watching a movie or playing a computer game, don't forget to turn off your DVD player or game console as well as the television itself.

Mobile energy

Your mobile phone charger uses more energy than you think. Much of the energy used by the phone chargers in the UK is wasted since they are only charging phones for a small part of the time they are actually plugged in. If everyone unplugged mobile phone chargers when the batteries are re-charged then the electricity saved could power 66,000 homes for a year!

Some effort:

• Check owners' manuals to make sure you're taking full advantage of any energy-conservation capabilities of your electronics.

• Be power-wise with your PC. Most personal computers have management features that control energy use. Turn your monitor off when you leave your computer, and activate its energy-saving features; this will reduce the energy it uses significantly.

• Switch your computer to sleep mode or turn it off completely if you think you will be away from it for more than an hour. Screensavers are not really energy savers and they may even use more than when the computer is in use.

- Think before you print:
  - Print only when you really need to – this saves energy, paper and ink and of course money.
  - Double-sided printing will save paper.
  - If your computer has 'draft' or 'economy' settings, use them to save ink.
- Extend the life of your electronics with proper care (Source: **www.mygreenelectronics.com**):
  - Review you owner's manuals for cleaning and maintenance of all products.
  - Take care of your products' insides. Never block or cover the ventilation areas of your electronics – these holes keep the product from overheating, which could shorten its life. Also, never stack components on top of one another.
  - Keep electronics out of direct sunlight and away from heaters and radiators. Likewise, keep out of areas with high humidity or dust.

More effort:
- Keep equipment for longer. For example:
  - Think about how often you really need to change your mobile phone – most phones will work for at least five years. Perhaps not the trendiest option, but it will reduce the risk from pollution by cadmium from discarded mobiles and probably save you money.
  - Don't assume you need a new monitor when you buy a new computer: monitors contain toxic chemicals which are hard to dispose of safely but don't need replacing as often.
- Watch less TV!

Turn off TV power

The average TV viewing time in America and Britain is four hours a day – half the time you are not sleeping or working. British children spend considerably longer watching TV than their European counterparts. That is a huge commitment of time. An organization called White Dot (**www.whitedot.org**) is campaigning against this lifestyle trend. They hope to increase awareness of how much time we lose by watching TV and the power of the TV industry to influence our thoughts, feelings and behaviour. Imagine what you could do with an extra 21–28 hours per week, not to mention the energy you would save!

Small cost actions

- Buy monitoring devices to check how much energy all your equipment uses – you may be surprised by how much some things use. For example, a broadband router left on all day can use as much energy as a fridge. See Chapter 02 for more information about monitoring equipment.
- Switch to rechargeable batteries. Many home electronic goods use batteries that require energy and resources to make, and can contain toxic chemicals that cause pollution if they're not disposed of properly. Switching to rechargeable batteries will save you money, save energy and reduce pollution. Buy NiMH (nickel metal hydride) rechargeable batteries – they last longer and are less harmful to the environment than older nickel cadmium (NiCD) batteries.

Batty batteries

The energy needed to make a battery can be 50 times more than the electrical energy it gives out!

- Wind-up or solar gadgets like radios and torches allow you to dispense with batteries altogether. They also avoid the frustration of things running out of power at the most inconvenient moments.
- Give your existing PC a new lease of life. Many computers are replaced every two or three years even though they still work; consider increasing your computer's memory (RAM) or replacing the hard drive instead.

Investment actions

Televisions

TVs account for a significant amount of the energy used in homes, so buying an energy-efficient TV can make a real difference. Consider the following suggestions to reduce their impact:

- In general, smaller TVs use less electricity.
- Look for the 'Energy Saving Recommended' logo (see Figure 2.4) when you purchase an integrated digital television (IDTV). It guarantees that the product is the most energy efficient in its category. See Energy Savings Trust website (**www.energysavingtrust.org.uk**) or call 0800 512 012 (free).

- A few models carry the European Ecolabel, which indicates a TV that consumes less energy during use and standby, contains fewer substances that are dangerous for health and the environment, and is designed to be easily recycled. See **www.eco-label.com**.
- Use the gadget 'TV Power Saver' which, when plugged between the mains socket and the television, claims to reduce 70–98 per cent of the standby energy used when switching it off using a remote control. See **www.evengreener.com** for further information.

TV switch to digital

The latest integrated digital televisions (IDTVs) receive digital TV without the need for a set-top box. This means they do the same as a TV plus a set-top box but with one power supply rather than two. Unlike many set-top boxes, IDTVs can be switched off without losing their settings and so don't have to be left on standby. The digital switch-over is due to take place between 2008 and 2012.

There are over 7 million terrestrial digital TV receivers in the UK, and if these were upgraded to IDTVs, this would save £45 million in energy bills. (Source: Energy Saving Trust.)

Computers

Consider the following suggestions:

- When buying a new computer, ask the retailer about Energy Star compliance for computers, monitors, fax machines and scanners.
- Consider a laptop – they are more energy efficient, only using about one sixth of the energy of a desktop computer in operation.
- UK-based Tranquil PC have recently launched a new fanless PC system, the T7, which uses just 15 watts of power, the same as a low energy light bulb.
- Make use of Microsoft's latest version of Windows 'sleep state' facility which uses 'absolute minimal' energy. Thirty per cent of PCs are left on overnight, 20 per cent over the weekend. (Source: Planet Ark, **www.planetark.com** 03/05/07.)

Green googling

Search engine giant Google and US firm Intel have joined an ambitious scheme to cut carbon dioxide emissions associated with computer use. Computers and other IT equipment may cause as much global warming as the airline industry. The plan sets out an industry-wide goal of reducing the amount of energy computers consume by 2010 by 54 million tonnes a year, the equivalent to the energy use of over 10 million cars.

The initiative builds on the World Wildlife Fund's Climate Savers programme, which helps companies to reduce their harmful greenhouse gas emissions. Other companies that have signed up include Hewlett-Packard, Dell and Microsoft, Yahoo, Hitachi and Sun Microsystems.

It is predicted that energy-efficient computers will be slightly more expensive but these costs would be offset by lower electricity bills. In addition, retailers will be encouraged to offer rebates to consumers who buy the 'green PCs'.

Meanwhile, in the UK, a new government taskforce has been formed to develop individual computers which use 98 per cent less energy than standard PCs.

Gadgets

There is an ever-increasing range of eco-friendly products available which help you cut down the energy you use, reduce your contribution to climate change and may save you money. Here are some of them:

- **Muscle powered gadgets** – There are now an array of 'wind-up' products that convert mechanical power into electricity, removing the need to replace or charge up batteries. Look for:
  - Phone chargers – a 45 second wind up powers your phone for several hours of standby.
  - Radios powered by a wind-up handle, every turn giving you about 1 minute of power.
  - Torches based on LED technology which convert human wind-up energy into light.
- Use a 'SavaPlug' – This replaces the normal plug on your fridge or freezer and limits the power drawn when the motor is running, but allows full power when needed.

- **One-click intelligent mains panel** – Automatically powers all your computer peripherals but stops them drawing unnecessary power when your computer is not in use. Recommended by the Energy Saving Trust and has received a number of excellent reviews. (See **www.oneclickpower.co.uk** for more information.)
- **Sensor lights** – This sensor activates your lights when you're in the room but switches them off automatically after you leave the room to save energy.
- **Solar chargers** – Using sunlight, these are available for battery chargers, iPods, mobile phones and garden lights.

Spreading the load!

There is new technology being developed to help reduce the amount of electricity used by appliances like fridges and freezers to help manage peaks in energy consumption. The appliances would have small electronic controllers installed to track peak times on the electricity grid, helping to reduce demand. This could provide a more stable and efficient grid, removing some of the barriers to more renewable electricity generation in the UK which tends to be highly variable. It is estimated that this technology could eventually save an estimated two million tonnes of CO_2 emissions a year when fully integrated across the network.

For more information see a new report from the Business, Enterprise and Regulatory Reform (BERR – **www.berr.gov.uk**) department.

Standby
Don't switch off – standby for the facts, then switch off!

- Seven out of ten people leave electrical devices on standby according to the Energy Savings Trust and at any one time the average household has up to 12 gadgets on standby or charging.
- Even when your devices are on standby they are still consuming energy and producing carbon emissions. Standby power can range between 10 and 15 watts, and if half a dozen devices are on standby, it is the equivalent of a 60 watt bulb.

(Following facts from: Tip the Planet – **www.tiptheplanet.com**.)

- Some TVs in standby mode use up to 85% of the power they use when switched on.
- Typically a TV is left on standby for 17.5 hours a day.
- One computer left on all day is responsible for 1,500 pounds (lbs) of CO_2 in a year. It would take 100 to 500 trees to absorb that amount of extra carbon dioxide released into the atmosphere.
- Stereos on standby cost £290 million and produce 1.6 million tonnes of CO_2.
- VCRs and DVDs cost £263 million and produce 1.06 million tonnes of CO_2.
- Currently the British Government are thinking of outlawing the use of electrical appliance standby modes, meaning manufacturers would have to change the design of such appliances in the UK.

There are some very new products around that claim to significantly reduce energy used for appliances whilst on stand by:

- The StandByPlug™ (www.standbyplug.co.uk) – An electrical device that automatically turns off an appliance that is in standby mode. The sensor detects the small drop in power and after a short while the trip switch shuts the appliance off completely.
- Bye Bye Standby is a set of power adaptors which you simply plug into your wall socket and then plug in your appliance. A single (remote control) switch can turn EVERYTHING off in one go. Look on it as 'central locking' for the home! Available as a starter pack from Domia (see http://www.domia.eu/).
- Sky box that goes to sleep – for those times we forget to switch everything off. Sky has introduced a clever new feature that will automatically switch Sky HD and Sky+ boxes into standby overnight.
- PSX2 – Goodbye Standby – With the PSX2 you can plug in several (or just one) device(s) and then when the PSX senses that they are no longer being used it cleverly shuts down the standby of each of the items. In the morning, you get up, point a remote control (any remote will do) at the PSX and it wakes everything back up again.

Savings summary

table 4.9 financial and environmental savings (computers, TVs and gadgets)

Action	Annual financial savings (£)	Annual energy savings (kWh)	Annual CO_2 savings (kg)
Turn off standby on multiple appliances (also includes power supply type plugs)	33	326	173[1]
Unplug chargers not in use	6	62	33
Upgrade TV to an IDTV	4	38	20[2]
Replacing an old television with an eco-labelled television	6	57	30[3]

Notes:

- Assume $0.53 kgCO_2/kWh$ for electricity consumption at a cost of 10p/kWh.
- CO_2 emission savings – source:
  - [1]Act on CO_2 calculator, 2007 (**http://actonco2.direct.gov.uk/**)
  - [2]Energy Saving Trust
  - [3]**www.mycarbonfootprint.eu** (calculator produced by European Commission – the calculator clearly defines the assumptions for figure).

Lighting

No cost actions

- Turn lights off if you leave a room for more than a few minutes.
- Make use of natural daylight wherever possible by:
  - opening curtains
  - keeping window ledges clear of clutter
  - reducing external obstacles that could block incoming light, e.g. by keeping trees and shrubs in the garden trimmed.
- Keep things clean. Dirt on walls can reduce their reflectability, and dust on lamps and fixtures can reduce the light shining through by almost half.
- Direct light to where it is needed.
- When planning a kitchen, try and place work surfaces near windows to reduce the need for artificial lighting.

A 100W light bulb left on for half an hour creates enough CO_2 to fill a party balloon. In the UK, 920,000 tonnes of CO_2, enough to fill 180,000 hot air balloons, is produced every year by lights being switched on unnecessarily. This costs us £140 million a year! (Source: Energy Saving Trust.)

Low cost actions

- Avoid high-wattage 'uplighters', which may use bulbs of 300W or more – use energy-efficient spotlights instead.
- Choose lampshades carefully – if too dark, they will reduce light from the bulb. A reflective surface provides a good quality diffused light.
- Have a candlelit dinner – save energy and be romantic!
- Avoid dark colours on ceilings as they absorb more light and so make it more likely that you will need to use artificial light.
- If you need to cover your windows for privacy, use light-coloured, loose-weave curtains to allow daylight to penetrate the room. Also, when decorating, choose lighter colours that reflect daylight.

- Avoid external floodlights that typically use 300–500W tungsten halogen lamps. These are not appropriate for most domestic settings where lighting is only required for short periods, such as lighting a path while in use. A 150W incandescent lamp (or in some cases a lower energy compact fluorescent lamp if lighting is required for longer periods) is usually sufficient, and will also avoid polluting the night sky and dazzling your neighbours every time the pet cat strolls by. You can also include a photocell to avoid them coming on in daylight and provide a presence detector.

- Replace traditional bulbs with energy-efficient ones. Changing all your light bulbs to the energy-saving kind is one of the easiest ways to save a lot of energy and money over the medium to long term. The initial higher cost is now far less significant as prices have come down over recent years. Just one drawback – you cannot use low energy light bulbs with a dimmer switch. The greatest savings will be in rooms that are lit for the longest such as the hall, lounge and landing. But these comparisons may all be redundant as there are plans to stop the supply of traditional bulbs for all EU countries, including the UK.

- Buy low energy light fittings that only take low energy light bulbs. They control the supply of electricity to the bulb, allowing for a small surge of power for a millisecond to light the bulb and then reducing the electricity flow to a very low level (source: Energy Savings Trust).

How low energy light bulbs work

Traditional bulbs waste a lot of their energy by turning it into heat rather than light. Low energy light bulbs work in the same way as fluorescent lights, an electric current passes through gas in a tube, making the tube's coating glow brightly. This means that they use less energy, as indicated in the table below, and are cool to the touch. Energy-saving bulbs have improved considerably over the years with a wide variety of styles and wattages and fittings available; so it's even easier to find an energy-efficient option. There have also been improvements in technology allowing 'instant start up' (as opposed to the traditional warm up period associated with low-energy bulbs), and warmer tones from the light itself which avoid the harsh white light traditionally associated with these bulbs.

Traditional bulbs	Energy-saving equivalent
25W	6W
40W	8–11W
60W	13–18W
100W	20–25W

Fading out traditional light bulbs

Traditional light bulbs could be taken off the shelves of UK shops within three years (of 2007) and replaced with energy-saving alternatives, the Government has said. It is expected that the European Commission will bring forward a proposal within three years for a minimum standard to prevent the sale of the least energy-efficient products within the EU. This will include commercial and domestic lighting.

The UK Government has already been talking to retailers and manufacturers about replacing 'inefficient' goods such as traditional light bulbs. An agreement on minimum standards may even come in before the EU sets laws on such items resulting in the removal of inefficient lighting products from UK shelves in advance of European regulations.

Savings summary

table 4.10 financial and environmental savings (lighting)

Action	Cost (£)	Annual financial savings (£)	Payback (yrs)	Lifespan of bulb (yrs)	Lifetime savings (£)	Annual CO₂ savings (kg)	Lifetime CO₂ savings for action (tonnes)	£ spent/ tonne CO₂ saved
Switch off five 60W lights	0	55	n/a	10+	548	290	2.9	n/a
Replace five 60 Watt bulbs with low energy bulbs (15 Watt)	15	41	0.4	10+	411	218	2.1	7
Replace five 100 Watt bulbs with low energy bulbs (20 Watt)	15	73	0.2	10+	730	387	3.8	4

Notes:

- Purchase costs based on Tesco supermarket offer (August 2007): part of the 'We're in this Together' campaign (www.together.com).

- Assume each lamp is used for five hours every day of the year.

- Assume $0.53kgCO_2$/kWh for electricity consumption at a cost of 10p/kWh.

Keeping cool

Climate change predictions are that we are going to see increasingly hot summers and periods of intense heat across the UK. Heatwaves claim thousands of lives, killing more people each year than floods, tornadoes and hurricanes combined, and it is going to get worse. Scientists calculate that as global warming bites and average temperatures around the world get higher, the risk of extreme heatwaves will also increase. The World Meteorological Organization estimates that the number of heat-related deaths across the globe will double in the next 20 years. The latest climate models suggest that the summer of 2003 will be the norm in Europe by the 2040s. For those countries that are not well adapted to dealing with excessively high temperatures, the consequences could be catastrophic. Unlike our continental neighbours, most of the homes in the UK are poorly designed for hot weather.

See Chapter 01 for more information on the impacts of global warming.

Air-conditioning – solution or problem?

It is ironic that the increasingly common approach to addressing the over-heating problems caused by climate change, namely air-conditioning, will only further add to the problem. Air-conditioning units are energy-guzzling systems adding to CO_2 levels and, therefore, fuelling further global warming. Sales of air-conditioners soared during the hot summer of 2006.

Using air-conditioning is not necessarily the answer. Air-con units are the least energy efficient of all cooling systems, are expensive to buy and expensive to run. Many use as much energy in one hour as a fridge-freezer does in a full day. A recent 'Which?' survey found that many 'A' rated models do not actually meet this standard in practice, using far more energy than you might expect. To make matters worse, most of the models currently being sold use hydrofluorocarbons (HFCs) as refrigerants, which can also add to global warming. (You may be able to find models that use a hydrocarbon, propane-based refrigerant as a preferable alternative, such as R290.)

Other problems with air-conditioning are:

- they can actually make rooms too cold
- the air filters need to be regularly changed
- the noise from the motors can be annoying.

There are many alternative options identified below – at least try them first!

No cost actions

- Keep windows, doors, curtains and blinds closed during the hottest part of the day (11 a.m.–3 p.m.), particularly those that are south-facing, to prevent solar gain.

- Open windows and doors to create a cooling draught before temperatures pick up in the day and in the evening when they have cooled back down. This can be extended during the night to really cool down the building and contents, which will give you a head start the following day. This approach can lower temperatures by up to 5°C, as much as you can expect from a typical air-conditioning unit, but at no cost and no pollution.

- Remember to turn fans off as soon as they have done the job.

- Stay downstairs as much as possible if you have more than one floor – hot air rises, so it is usually cooler on lower floors.

- Wear loose and light-coloured clothing to allow air to move more freely around your body or to be reflected away.

If you do have air-conditioning

- Set your thermostat temperature as high as comfortably possible in hot periods.

- There is no advantage in setting your thermostat at a colder setting than usual when you first turn on your air-conditioner. It will not speed up the cooling of your home and could result in excessive cooling and, therefore, a waste of energy and money.

- Don't place the air-conditioning thermostat near 'warm' spots, such as near appliances and lights. The thermostat will sense the heat from these appliances, and therefore the air-conditioner may run for longer than necessary.

- Maintain the air-conditioner by keeping the filter and cooling coil clean, and thereby allowing it to run more efficiently and use less energy.

Low cost actions

- Use fans – they are cheap to buy and economical to run. Fans provide a cooling effect by moving air around (draughts) rather than reducing actual room temperature.

- Shade south-facing windows with tight fitting blinds made from a fabric called 'black out' or by fitting external shutters.
- Insulate the hot water cylinder to prevent it radiating heat into the house. You can buy a jacket for your hot water cylinder from your local DIY store. This is also one of the simplest and cheapest things you can do to cut your fuel bills and save energy (see earlier section in this chapter on 'Hot water').

Investment actions

- Paint your house a light colour so that heat is reflected away – this approach is commonly used in Mediterranean countries.
- Install light-coloured awnings to reduce heat gain in your home.
- Replace carpets with ceramic tiles – the Mediterranean approach to hot summers.
- Plant trees and shrubs to shade hot rooms. However, this may need to be balanced with the benefit of letting in light and making heat gains in the winter months.

Cooling plants!

The US Department of Energy estimates that just three trees, properly placed around the house, can save an average household between $100 and $250 in energy costs annually. To be most effective, trees should be located on the south and west sides of your home. Deciduous trees will shade in summer and allow light and radiant heat to pass through in the winter. Choose varieties which are native to your environment, fast growing and tall enough to be effective.

The arbor is a traditional cooling method used worldwide. Arbors placed along the sides of the house will reduce temperatures as the air passes through the arbor and is cooled by the plant's leaves. The shade created by the arbor is also beneficial.

Climbing plants provide shading and cooling, and are quick to grow. Trellises should be placed on the hottest side of the house, at least 6 inches (approximately 18 cm) from the wall to protect the wall and provide a buffer of cool air. Certain climbers, such as deciduous clematis and wisteria, will even grow well in containers if open ground is unavailable.

Shrubs shade walls from heat gain by blocking sunlight. They also act as a windbreak in winter to help protect the house from cold air. Choose shrubs which are low maintenance and grow to a fixed height. Native varieties will do best.

Take care to plant trees and shrubs where their roots will be clear of underground wires, sewer lines, septic tanks or house foundations. (Source: Tip the Planet – **www.tiptheplanet.com**.)

Teenage consumers

Teenagers are often seen as self-indulgent, unthinking, wasteful and careless about energy use. It is certainly true that teenagers have a tendency to bathe more (hence increased hot water and energy use), have more gadgets to plug in and charge, and are not as attentive to turning off lights as their grumpy bill-paying parents (See Table 4.11 and Figure 4.21).

table 4.11 the young technophile annual cost (Source: Energy Saving Trust report – 'The ampere strikes back – How consumer electronics are taking over the world')

Gadget	Running cost
PS3	£23
14″ CRT in bedroom	£6.50
Freeview STB	£6
1 Mobile phone – personal	£0.50
Digital radio	£5
iPod	£0.50
VCR	£11
PC and monitor	£29.50
Printer	£2.50
Scanner	£5
PC speakers	£3
Compact hi-fi	£8.50
Total annual running cost	**£101**

figure 4.21 the teenage consumer (© Hockerton Housing Project)

However, rather than creating a battleground between teens and parents, some clear rules and subtle education may be more productive. At the risk of fanning family strife, here are some suggestions:

- Take the time to explain to your children the link between energy use, bills and the impact on the environment. They have probably covered this at school and so should be fairly familiar with the concept, indeed they may start to lecture you! You could even involve them in monitoring energy use around the home.

- Focus on those things that will really make a difference, rather than picking teenagers up on everything. You are more likely to get cooperation, and eventually you may be able to extend your discussions to more areas. The big areas are likely to be the amount of hot water they use for washing and the heating in their bedroom.

- Set the hot water programmer so that there is a focused time of the day when most people are happy to shower/bathe. This will use energy more efficiently since the hot water does not need to be available for quite so long. It will also mean that the bathroom is far warmer for most of the family and may reduce the tendency to run showers to pre-heat the bathroom.

- Encourage teenagers to get involved practically with any DIY improvements – they will one day be paying energy bills of their own and they may then thank you for the free training.

- Encourage family meals and other activities together. It may sound old fashioned, and may disrupt the viewing of 'EastEnders', but it could save energy by reducing the amount of time some rooms need to be heated in the evening and by switching off one or more TVs. You never know, you may all learn to enjoy it more (in the end!).

- Reduce the number of TVs in the house – try and encourage family viewing.

- Have a central place in the home for charging mobile phones and other equipment. This will help to avoid several chargers sitting about the house all plugged in to sockets but not actually charging anything.

- Avoid allowing your teenager to have their own fridge in the bedroom, unless they are renting it as a bed-sit and covering their share of the energy bills.

- Replication of electrical appliances and gadgets in the name of independence will only increase energy use and, ultimately, your bills.

- Appeal to your teenager's idealism by encouraging them to become active and campaigning. They could join:
  - The Green Party – for students and anyone still in full-time education this costs just £5. (See teen section of Green Party website http://www.younggreens.org.uk/TeenGreens.)
  - Friends of the Earth (see www.foe.co.uk or call 020 7490 1555).
  - See http://www.teenissues.co.uk/LivingAGreenLife.html.

- Inspire them by taking them to places such as:
  - Centre for Alternative Technology, Powys, Wales (see **www.cat.org.uk**).
  - Hockerton Housing Project (see **www.hockertonhousing-project.org.uk**).
  - Many more options to discover in *Eco-Centres and Courses*, by Terena Plowright (published by Green Books, Totnes **www.greenbooks.co.uk**).
- They could read *You Can Save The Planet – A Day in the Life of Your Carbon Footprint* (Rich Hough). Published by Guardian Books (call 0870 836 0749 or see **www.guardianbooks.co.uk**) at £8.99, this book is aimed at children and teenagers, taking them through the environmental baddies hidden in an average day.

Moving home

Moving home can have consequences for your environmental impact. Where you choose to live in relation to work, school and recreational facilities will determine how much you need to travel. The type and condition of the property will affect how much energy you need to use to make it comfortable. Moving house is also a great opportunity to think about what changes you wish to make to the property and how to kit it out to reduce your future energy use. On the other hand, if you are selling a property, improving the energy efficiency of your home could encourage buyers. The following are just a few pointers to think about when moving home:

- **Energy ratings for new homes**
  In most cases now, if you are purchasing a house your seller is required to provide you with an Energy Performance Certificate as part of a Home Information Pack. This provides valuable information about the strengths and weaknesses of the property from an energy perspective, with suggestions for improvements. (For further information see Chapter 02.)
- **Insulation and heating**
  The heating and hot water requirements of a modern house account for about 80 per cent of its energy use. Therefore, focus on these aspects of the home to save energy and money. How good is the insulation? Ask about the wall and loft

insulation – why not check the roof space yourself, rather
than relying on a surveyor? How old is the boiler, what type
is it, and when was it last serviced? If the boiler is older than
ten years it is likely to be far less efficient than new
condensing models. (For further information see beginning of
this chapter – 'Keeping warm'.)

When you do finally move in, make sure you have been
instructed on how to use the heating controls or have been
given any available manuals. Ensure also that you are given
any relevant guarantees. If you are selling a home it is
important that you also do the same for the people moving
into your home.

Add value to your home

Research commissioned by the Energy Saving Trust, and carried
out by IPSOS Mori in January 2006, shows that buyers are willing
to pay up to £10,000 more for an environmentally-friendly home.
More than two thirds look beyond cosmetic details to more
important factors, such as the condition of the boiler or the quality
of the windows. Rising fuel prices and greater environmental
awareness are encouraging buyers to consider a home's running
costs and its impact on the planet.

• **Appliances, furniture and fittings**
  When you move home you are likely to need to purchase new
  appliances and other items, and so this is an ideal time to
  select products that have a reduced environmental impact.
  Look out for energy labels, and in particular the 'Energy
  Saving Recommended' logo on many products, which is your
  guarantee that they are the most efficient in their class (see
  Chapter 02 for further information). They may cost a bit
  more, but this is quickly paid off with great savings on
  energy. Other things to consider:
  – Switch to energy efficient light bulbs. The savings add up
    very quickly. (See 'Lighting' section earlier in this chapter.)
  – Consider buying second-hand, or renovating items like
    furniture and curtains. It helps to save raw materials and
    energy, and will also cut waste.
  – When buying timber products like furniture or flooring,
    check they are from a sustainable source and carry the
    Forestry Stewardship Commission (FSC) label.

- **Transport**

  Private cars produce around 13 per cent of the UK's carbon emissions. When looking for a new home, consider how you can reduce the distance you will need to travel by car. Choosing a location with good public transport links can help you cut your car journeys. Reducing your car fuel usage saves you money and helps to save the planet. (For further information on greener travelling, see Chapter 07.)

05

generating your own energy

In this chapter you will learn:
- the best options for microgeneration
- practicalities of installation
- what are the likely performances and paybacks
- about possible funding sources
- what is a ROC?

Introduction

Generating your own energy is often referred to as **microgeneration**, the small-scale generation of low-carbon heat and/or electricity. You may also hear the term **renewables**, referring to energy which is regenerated 'naturally' over a short timescale. Various technologies exist for generating renewable energy, such as solar thermal, photovoltaic cells (PVs), wind power, hydropower and biomass.

It is likely that microgeneration will become increasingly popular as more people take personal action to reduce growing household energy use and costs. For some, the motivation is to ensure reliable energy supplies to their homes. There are also a number of factors making it easier and more attractive to generate your own energy:

- An improved range of more reliable, smaller, flexible units, better suited for homes.
- The greater availability of some of the technologies for the average householder to purchase, including DIY stores that now stock a variety of products, such as solar panels and even wind turbines.
- Grants of up to 50 per cent available from the Government, utilities and other sources that reduce the high initial costs of installation. Funding is likely to be reduced, however, in the medium to long term, but this will hopefully be offset by a general decrease in retail prices as supply and demand increases.
- Easing of planning restrictions. In recent years the Government has been trying to enable more households to install small-scale microgeneration technologies, including solar panels and small wind turbines, by reducing planning restrictions. This is not always well supported by local planning authorities, but at least the trend is encouraging.
- Government plans to legislate for a steady escalation of Building Regulations towards 'zero carbon' standards for new housing that will require increasing contributions by renewables or low-carbon technology. The aim is that by 2017 all new housing developments will have to able to generate as much energy on site as the homes use in total.
- Additional income opportunities, such as ROCs (see later). Other countries pay as much as three times their current electricity tariff for solar power provided to the grid, making the finances far more appealing.
- Rising energy prices in the medium to long term.

Off-the-shelf power kits

Some retailers have recognized the potential explosive growth in interest for microgeneration products from consumers. Curry's started to sell solar panels in some of its stores in 2007, for £1,000. They offer an in-store consultation followed by a free home assessment to check that the property is suitable. B&Q launched the sale of roof-mounted wind turbines and solar thermal panels in early 2007.

General guidance

The variables are unique to each household and each set of circumstances; however, there are some general rules.

- **GOLDEN RULE:** *Only* **consider microgeneration when you have taken all measures possible to reduce the energy consumption in your home.** (See Chapter 03 which discusses this in the context of a strategic approach and Chapter 04 which recommends specific energy-saving actions.)
- Location and siting is critical and suitability will vary depending on which form of microgeneration technology you are considering. Suppliers should provide much of this advice, but take independent professional advice if you have any doubts. Generally speaking, do not consider:
  - solar thermal (water heating) or solar PV (electricity) if the only available surface faces north, or if the panels would be in shadow for most of the day
  - a wind turbine if your average wind speed is below about 4 metres/second and/or you are surrounded by tall trees, hedges or buildings that act as a wind shelter
  - a ground source heat pump if you have a small garden.
- To maximize returns, whatever technology you are considering, it should be able to generate close to its potential maximum (the supplier should provide this) and it should be matched as close as possible to the demands of the household. For example, there is no point installing a solar thermal system to provide hot water, if you go away for most of the summer.
- Have early discussions with the local planning authority, especially if there is likely to be some visual or traffic impact.
- Make sure you get as much 'credit' as possible for the energy you generate – you will most likely use your microgeneration

system to complement your mains supply, thereby reducing the amount of grid electricity that you import and pay for. When your system is generating more electricity than you are using, the excess can be fed back (exported) to the national grid; and when the system is not generating enough for your needs, you can draw off your mains supply in the usual way. You should ask your electricity supplier about them paying for the electricity that your home exports to the grid (an arrangement known as net-metering). You can get paid even more via ROCs (see below) – a sort of bonus payment!

- Small-scale renewable energy systems can be the least-cost option in locations which do not have an existing grid connection and where energy demand is low.

- Obtain good independent advice. Your nearest Energy Saving Trust advice centre can tell you about accredited installers in your area for different types of microgeneration. Call freephone 0800 512 012 or see **www.energysavingtrust.org.uk**.

- Certification for products and installers is provided within the Governments 'Low Carbon Buildings Programme' – for further information see **www.ukmicrogeneration.org** or call 0845 6181514.

  - To find a certified installer call 0800 915 0990 or see the website: **www.lowcarbonbuildings.org.uk/info/installers/find/installerfind**.

  - To find a certified product see the website **www.clear-skies.org/Households/RecognisedProducts.aspx**.

- The Centre for Alternative Technology (CAT) (www.cat.org.uk) gives very good advice, how-to-do guides and runs courses for those wishing to generate their own electricity.

Doing the sums

The installation of any microgeneration system will have a significant cost, usually several thousands of pounds as a minimum. As with any financial investment, the decision to spend a large sum of money needs to involve an assessment of the rate of return on that investment. The formula below is an adaptation of that shown for payback in Chapter 01 ('Reduce energy costs') and Chapter 03 ('Payback time').

$$\text{Payback (number of years)} = \frac{\text{Capital cost } - \text{ Grants received}}{\text{Annual income (energy cost savings + ROCs)}}$$

(This does not allow for loss of interest or loss of opportunity to invest in something else.)

The energy cost savings = Energy generated (kWh) × unit cost of fuel replaced per kWh.

However, bear the following in mind:

- If you are not paid for energy that you export, or paid at a discounted rate, you will need to subtract the value from total savings.
- Energy prices are not constant. Depending on your contract tariffs, you are likely to be paying different rates for 'peak' and 'off-peak' times. This is likely to be less complicated for solar systems as it is only generated during the day when tariffs are at their highest.
- Replacing gas saves far less emissions and money as it is less carbon intensive and cheaper to purchase – this is more likely to affect solar thermal and ground source heat pumps that offset hot water and heating systems.
- The energy yield may not be as high as suggested by suppliers/installers and is likely to vary significantly through the year and between years.
- Any change in energy price could have a significant impact on savings and hence payback period – however, the long-term trend is for fuels to increase in price, and therefore making microgeneration financially more worthwhile.

When looking at the finances for microgeneration you may also hear the term or be quoted the Net Present Value (NPV), which is an estimate of the profitability of your investment, taking into account typical purchase costs and the value of future energy savings over the lifetime of the equipment. Internal Rate of Return (IRR) is closely linked to the NPV and is the return on investment expressed as an interest rate that you could earn from investing funds in home energy generation.

What is a ROC?

The Renewables Obligation (RO) and the Renewables Obligation Scotland (ROS) were introduced in April 2002 by the Government to encourage the development of renewable energy and help reduce carbon emissions by requiring electricity suppliers to produce a specified proportion of their power from renewable generation annually or else pay a penalty. The Government intends that suppliers will be subject to a renewables obligation until 31 March 2027. The amount is also set to increase annually.

Suppliers are required to produce evidence of their compliance of the scheme by producing green certificates referred to as **Renewable Obligation Certificates** or **ROCs**. Each ROC is equivalent to one megawatt hour (1,000,000 units) of renewable electricity generated.

Electricity companies that fall short of targets can reduce penalty costs by purchasing ROCs from other generators, including small producers such as householders. These then become a traded commodity with generators selling their ROCs to electricity companies/suppliers providing an annual income. This would be in addition to revenue received on all exported units of electricity, and so can really help reduce payback time. See Table 5.1 towards the end of this chapter, which includes examples of photovoltaic systems with and without ROCs income – it can almost halve the payback period.

ROCs are bought and sold in the market place by large generators, traders, brokers and electricity suppliers. Market prices vary on a daily basis, currently at a value of 4–4.5p/kWh, providing a premium of about 40–50 per cent on top of normal electricity prices. To see recent ROC prices see the website **http://www.nfpa.co.uk/**. It does not matter if you consume all or part of the electricity produced. The electricity generated, classified as 'eligible own use', is potentially eligible for ROCs, whether it is used by your home, a third party or exported to the grid.

To obtain ROCs, you as a 'generator', need to be accredited by Ofgem (**www.ofgem.gov.uk**). For small operators (such as a householder), this process is usually far too complex. Instead you can go via an intermediary (e.g. the 'green' electricity supplier, Good Energy) who will complete the accreditation form on your behalf. Certain site specific information will be required for the application and you will need to ensure that your meter is one certified by Ofgem. An agreement between the generator owner and the electricity supplier, such as a 'buy and sell back' may need to be put in place in order for the generator to qualify for ROC accreditation.

Further resources:

- **Good Energy** (**www.good-energy.co.uk** or call 0845 456 1640) will act as an intermediary and pay per unit of electricity generated through their renewable energy device. They also retire ROCs over and above the level required by law, which helps to increase the market value and the prices renewable generators receive for their ROCs.

- **Trade Link Solutions Ltd** (**www.tradelinksolutions.com**) provide a range of services including independent advice. They also project manage the operations of several small renewable projects on a day to day basis which includes the buying, selling and trading of ROCs on behalf of clients.

More ROCs

Good Energy is an energy supplier with a difference. All the electricity they provide is from renewables and they are particularly keen to support independent renewable energy generators. Acting as an intermediary, via their 'Homegen' scheme, they buy up the ROC equivalents from small generators, and as of 1 October 2007 they have doubled this to 9p a unit, approximately double the normal rate for ROCs.

In some countries, such as Germany, they pay small generators as much as three times electricity prices as an incentive – will the UK and other countries follow this?

Funding

The Government is offering grants for microgeneration technologies which can cover up to 50 per cent of the costs for solar photovoltaics, and up to 30 per cent for other technologies, such as wind turbines, solar thermal and heat pumps. This is part of the Department of Trade and Industry's (DTI) funded 'Low Carbon Buildings Programme' which started in April 2006 and will run over three years. Individual property owners including private householders can apply but, to qualify for a grant, your home needs to fulfill certain criteria. For instance, you already need to be using energy-saving light bulbs throughout your house, have a thermostat on your heating system, and have sufficient loft and cavity insulation. You will also need to use a certified installer and products. Further details can be found on the website **www.lowcarbonbuildings.org.uk** or call 0800 915 0990.

The 'Scottish Community Householder Renewables Initiative' (SCHRI) provides grants for properties in Scotland. This is funded by the Scottish Executive and managed by the Energy Saving Trust. Grants are available for solar water heating, solar thermal space heating, small scale wind and hydro systems, ground source heat pumps, air source heat pumps and biomass. Funding for householders is set at 30 per cent of the installed cost up to £4,000. If you live in Scotland, you can choose to have a SCHRI or a low carbon buildings programme grant. However, you can only apply for one grant per technology from either of these programmes. See the SCHRI website (**www.energysavingtrust.org.uk/schri/**) for more information or call the SCHRI Hotline on 0800 138 8858.

The Environment and Renewable Energy Fund provides renewable energy grants for householders in Northern Ireland. See the website **www.actionrenewables.org/site/** for more information or call 0800 023 4077 (free).

Further grants or funding may be possible from utility companies (such as Scottish Power) who have set up specific funding programmes focused particularly on community initiatives. These are likely to be extended in future years, possibly to the individual householder.

The options

Quick guide to options

(No ranking is implied. Site location will normally dictate the choice of technology.)

- **Solar water heating (solar thermal)** uses solar panels to capture heat from the sun and provide domestic hot water. Solar water heating is suitable for urban and rural environments.
- **Photovoltaic cells (PVs)/Solar PV** use solar panels to generate electricity to run appliances and lighting. They can be free-standing in arrays, or incorporated into roofing materials, glazing or wall cladding. Solar PV is suitable for urban and rural environments.

- **Small wind turbines (microwind)** are usually more cost effective than photovoltaics when there is a reasonable wind resource. They can power a single dwelling, a business or community building, or even a whole community. They can be incorporated onto buildings (usually roof-mounted) or be free standing on a tower. Wind speed and consistency are critical, which limits good locations, particularly in built up areas.

- **Ground source heat pumps (geothermal)** take heat from under the ground using liquid circulating in pipes, to deliver space heating and, in some cases, to pre-heat domestic hot water. There are also other types of heat pumps less commonly available; air source (use warm air, e.g. from a glazed sunspace) and water source heat pumps (usually from a large body of water).

- **Hydro power** systems capture the energy in flowing water and convert it to electricity via a turbine. There is potential for small-scale hydro schemes where there is a reasonable flow and 'head' of river water. If successful it can be considerably more cost effective than other forms of microgeneration.

- **Biomass (biofuels)** refers to the burning of organic matter such energy crops, agricultural and forestry residues and plants to make energy or heat. Biofuels can be used in simple combustion processes to supply heat, usually using modern efficient wood-fired boilers that can be automated. They can also fuel more complex combined heat and power (CHP) schemes to generate electricity and distribute heat. During combustion processes, CO_2 is released that was previously locked up in the biofuel as it grew, making it effectively CO_2 neutral. Biofuel does not include fossil fuels, which have taken millions of years to evolve (e.g. coal).

Solar thermal

Of all the options for microgeneration, this is probably the most developed and accessible to householders, with a large choice of equipment available to suit many applications. It is most beneficial (financially and environmentally) for households that cannot use gas, particularly those reliant on electricity, or those that use large quantities of hot water. However, this does not necessarily mean that it is the most cost effective – see Table 5.1 towards the end of this chapter.

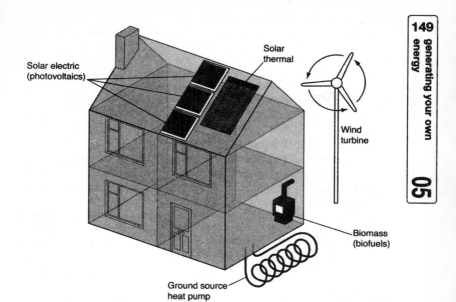

figure 5.1 microgeneration options for the home (© Hockerton Housing Project)

figure 5.2 solar thermal installation (Source: Solartwin – **www.solartwin.com**)

How it works (solar thermal):

There are three main components to a domestic system:

1 **Solar panels or collectors** – These are fitted to your roof and collect heat from the sun's radiation. There are two main types of collector:
   - Flat plate systems are comprised of an absorber plate with a transparent cover.
   - Evacuated tube systems are comprised of a row of glass tubes that each contains an absorber plate feeding into a manifold which then transports the heated fluid.
2 **A heat transfer system** – This transfers the collected heat to the water.
3 **Hot water cylinder** – This stores the hot water for use later on.

Practicalities (solar thermal):

- Solar water heating can provide around a third of your hot water needs over the course of a year (source: Energy Saving Trust).
- For maximum efficiency you will need a panel mounted on a southeast to southwest facing roof receiving direct sunlight for the main part of the day. A typical system is 3–4m^2 in size.
- You may need space for an additional water cylinder.
- A competent and accredited installer will be able to assess your situation and discuss with you the best system to meet your needs.
- Some combi boilers are not compatible with solar thermal systems.
- Solar hot water systems can be integrated into a new roof system as part of repair work, which would save on material costs and installation costs.
- Possible advantages with evacuated tube systems are that they can be mounted on a vertical surface, the individual tubes are rotated to be at the optimum angle for solar collection.
- The technology is generally highly reliable as the pump is the only moving part and rarely causes any problems. However, there are many products available and so it will be very much dependent on the system you purchase.

- There are a number of DIY solar thermal courses where you can learn how to build and install solar thermal systems at a much lower cost – for example, Low Impact Living Initiative (01296 714184, **www.lowimpact.org**) or try the Centre for Alternative Technology (CAT, **www.cat.org.uk**).

- It is hard to find information on the comparative performance of different solar systems to help make the best choice.

- A solar thermal system is likely to be a permitted development under local planning guidance.

Photovoltaic cells

Photovoltaic cells (PVs) or solar PVs use sunlight to produce electricity via semi-conductor technology. Although they are expensive, prices have fallen in recent years and are likely to continue to do so. They may also add value to your home if you decide to sell.

How they work (photovoltaic cells):

The PV cell consists of one or two layers of a semi-conducting material, usually silicon. When sunlight shines on the cell it creates an electric field across the layers causing electricity to flow. The greater the intensity of the light, the greater will be the flow of electricity. PV cells are referred to in terms of the amount of electricity they produce in full sunlight; known as kilowatt peak or kWp.

Practicalities (photovoltaic cells):

- It does not always need to be sunny for PVs to produce electricity; some power can still be generated even on a cloudy day. However, the more intense the sunlight, the more electricity is produced.

- You can use PV systems on a building with a roof or wall that faces within 90 degrees of south, as long as it is not over-shadowed by other buildings or large trees. This can sometimes present an issue in built up areas as shading will significantly reduce the output of the system.

- Solar panels are fairly heavy and so the roof must be strong enough to take their weight, especially if the panel is placed on top of existing tiles.

- PV arrays now come in a variety of shapes and colours to suit the location so that they need not be obtrusive. You can purchase grey 'solar tiles' that look like roof tiles and panels or transparent cells that can be used on conservatories and glass which will provide shading as well as generating electricity.

- Solar roof tiles (e.g. C21e) are available that actually replace conventional tiles and so can be installed by any roofer or competent individual. They can, however, be more expensive overall and there may be future issues if any wiring goes wrong since you may have to take part of the roof apart to repair it!

- Photovoltaic tile systems can be integrated into a new roof system as part of repair work, which would save on material costs and installation costs.

- Grid connected systems require very little maintenance. The panels need to be kept relatively clean and free from shading. The wiring and components of the system should, however, be checked regularly by a qualified technician.

- Stand-alone systems not connected to the grid will need maintenance on additional system components, such as batteries.

- A roof-mounted PV array is likely to be a permitted development under local planning guidance. However, you still need to check with your local authority, especially if you live in a conservation area or have a listed building.

figure 5.3 fitting PV panels to homes at Hockerton Housing Project (© Hockerton Housing Project)

Small wind turbines (microwind)

Most people are familiar with the sight of a wind farm, but you can also generate energy at home on a smaller scale with your own wind turbine (microwind). The UK has 40 per cent of Europe's total wind energy, but it is still largely untapped with only 0.5 per cent of our electricity requirements currently generated by wind power (source: Energy Saving Trust).

How they work (microwind):

Wind turbines use the wind's lift forces to rotate aerodynamic blades that turn a rotor creating electricity. Most small wind turbines generate direct current (DC) electricity. A special inverter and controller is needed to convert DC electricity to alternating current (AC) electricity at a quality and standard acceptable to the grid. No battery storage is required for grid-connected systems.

Practicalities (microwind):

- Individual turbines vary in size and power. Output ranges from a few hundred watts to two or three megawatts. Domestic systems typically range from 1–6 kilowatts.

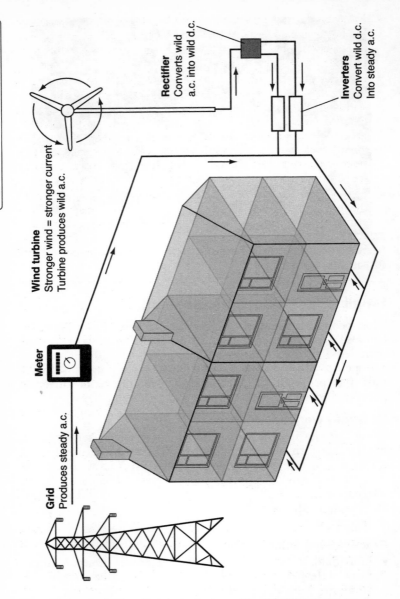

Wind turbine
Stronger wind = stronger current
Turbine produces wild a.c.

Rectifier
Converts wild
a.c. into wild d.c.

Inverters
Convert wild d.c.
Into steady a.c.

Meter

Grid
Produces steady a.c.

figure 5.4 typical microwind system set up with grid (© Hockerton Housing Project)

- Microwind ranges from very small turbines supplying energy for battery charging systems such as boats or electric fences, to larger turbines supplying small housing developments (e.g. Hockerton Housing Project).

- Electricity generated at any one time by a wind turbine is highly dependent on the speed and direction of the wind. The windspeed is itself dependent on a number of factors, such as location within the UK, the height of the turbine above ground level and the presence of nearby obstructions. The ideal site is a smooth top hill with a flat, clear exposure, free from excessive turbulence and obstructions such as large trees, houses or other buildings.

- Ideally, you should undertake a professional assessment of the local windspeed for a full year at the exact location where you plan to install a turbine before proceeding. In practice, this may be difficult, expensive and time-consuming. Generally, it is recommended that you only consider a wind turbine under the following circumstances:

  - The local annual average windspeed is six metres per second or more – an approximate figure for your location can be checked using the Department for Business, Enterprise & Regulatory Reform's (BERR) wind speed database – go to the website **www.berr.gov.uk** and search under 'windspeed database'.

  - There are no significant nearby obstacles such as buildings, trees or hills that are likely to reduce the windspeed or increase turbulence.

  If you are in any doubt, it is worthwhile consulting a suitably qualified professional.

- Wind turbines work best higher up where wind speed is greater. The turbines can either be mounted on a mast located near the building that will be using the electricity, or roof-mounted on the building itself. If you have enough space in a suitable location, a mast-mounted system is likely to produce a higher output. There may also be increased cost and practical problems with roof or wall-mounted turbines, particularly if reinforcing is required and particular care is need with lime mortar.

- Wind turbines will usually require planning permission and so check with your local authority. The main issues likely to be raised are visual impact, noise and impact on neighbouring house prices! Recent surveys have shown that the market value of local properties is not obviously affected.

- Small-scale wind power is particularly suitable for remote off-grid locations where conventional methods of supply are expensive or impractical. Systems that are not connected to the national grid require battery storage as well as an inverter to convert DC electricity to AC mains electricity.

- Turbines require service checks every few years to ensure they work efficiently. For battery storage systems, typical battery life is around six to ten years, depending on the type, so batteries are likely to need replacing at some point in the system's life.

Can we harvest useful wind energy from the roofs of our buildings?

Are you one of the many people who have read or heard that the next generation of roof-mounted wind turbines will provide much of the electricity needs of the average home in the UK? Renewable energy experts, including Government-funded agencies, have expressed concerns that roof-mounted turbines may not perform as well as initially expected. They are worried that many of them have not been adequately tested. Trials have since started in 2007, including the Warwick Microwind Trial project (see **www.warwickwindtrials.org.uk**). It was assumed that they would perform like larger wind turbines on masts sited in exposed areas, but air turbulence caused by obstructions such as neighbouring buildings and trees affects performance dramatically with wind speeds of four metres per second or less. The recommended minimum is an average of six metres per second, which is only likely in exposed areas or by using a mast.

Ground source heat pumps

This method of generation utilizes the natural heat of the earth. A few metres down, the soil in the UK maintains a heat of 11–12°C and by feeding a coil into the soil and transferring the heat from the ground into a building, heating and hot water can be produced. These systems can also be used for space cooling. For every unit of electricity used to operate the system, 3–4 units of heat are usually produced.

How they work (ground source heat pumps):

There are three important elements to a ground source heat pump (see Figure 5.5):

1 **The ground loop** – Lengths of pipe buried in the ground, either in a vertical borehole or a horizontal trench. The pipe is usually a closed circuit and is filled with a mixture of water and antifreeze. This is pumped around the pipe absorbing heat from the ground. The ground loop can be:
   * vertical, for use in boreholes (see Figure 5.5)
   * horizontal, for use in trenches
   * spiral, coil or 'slinky', also for use in trenches.

2 **A heat pump** – In the same way that your fridge uses refrigerant to extract heat from the inside to keep your food cool, a ground source heat pump extracts heat from the ground and then uses it to heat your home. The heat pump has three main parts:
   * The evaporator uses the refrigerant liquid in the ground loop to absorb the heat (like the squiggly thing in the cold part of your fridge).
   * The compressor moves the refrigerant round the heat pump and compresses it to the correct temperature for the heat distribution system (this is what makes the noise in your fridge).
   * The condenser gives up heat to a hot water tank which feeds the distribution system (like the hot part at the back of your fridge).

3 **Heat distribution system** – This consists of either under-floor heating or radiators for space heating and in some cases water storage for hot water supply.

Practicalities (ground source heat pumps):

* The efficiency of a ground source heat pump system is measured by the coefficient of performance (CoP). This is the ratio of units of heat produced for each unit of electricity used to drive the compressor and pump for the ground loop. Typical CoPs range from 3–4 (source: Energy Saving Trust). This means that for every unit of electricity used to operate the system, 3–4 units of heat are produced.

* If grid electricity is used for the compressor and pump, then it is worth shopping around amongst energy providers to benefit from the lowest running costs, for example, by choosing an economy 10 or economy 7 tariff.

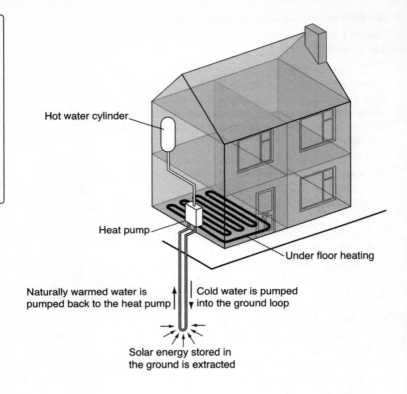

Hot water cylinder

Heat pump

Under floor heating

Naturally warmed water is
pumped back to the heat pump

Cold water is pumped
into the ground loop

Solar energy stored in
the ground is extracted

figure 5.5 ground source heat pump via borehole

- Ground source heat pumps are typically combined with under-floor heating. This type of heating system, unlike radiators, works with the lower water temperature produced by a ground source heat pump.
- It can be disruptive to install but for new developments it can be installed with other building works.
- Ground source heat pumps are not recommended if you are short of space as you will need space for a trench or borehole to accommodate the ground loop.
- Ground source heat pumps are most beneficial (financially and environmentally) for households that cannot use gas, particularly those reliant on electricity.

Air and water source heat pumps

Air and water source heat pumps use air or water respectively. They do not rely on a collection system and simply extract the heat from the source at the point of use.

Air source heat pumps can be fitted outside a house or in the roof space and generally perform better at slightly warmer air temperatures. Water source heat pumps can be used to provide heating in homes near to rivers, streams, lakes and lochs for example.

Hydro power

If you are lucky enough to have a river or even a small stream running through your property, then this could be a very effective means of generating power. Hydro power systems use running water to turn a turbine which produces electricity. A micro-hydro plant is one that generates less than 100kW. Improvements in small turbine and generator technology mean that micro-hydro schemes have become an attractive means of producing electricity.

How it works (hydro power):

- The potential energy of water held at height is converted to kinetic energy as it flows and turns a turbine which then produces electrical energy.
- The total energy available in a body of water will depend on the height (or head) that the water falls and the water's flow rate. Hydro systems are categorized as low head, medium head and high head.
- The scheme's actual output will depend on how efficiently it converts the power of the water into electrical power. Maximum efficiencies of over 90% are possible but for small systems 60–80 per cent is more realistic (source: Energy Saving Trust).

Practicalities (hydro power):

- Hydro power requires the water source to be relatively close to where the power will eventually be used or to a suitable grid connection.
- For houses with no mains connection but with access to a micro-hydro site, a good hydro system can generate a more reliable electricity supply than other renewable technologies at a lower cost. The peak energy season is during the winter months when larger quantities of electricity are required.

Total system costs can be high but they are often less than the cost of a grid connection (source: Energy Saving Trust).

- In off-grid systems the power is used for lighting and electrical appliances. Electricity can be supplied directly to the devices or through an inverter and battery store. When available power exceeds demand, space and water heating can also be supplied. A back-up power system may be needed to compensate for seasonal variations in water flow.
- Maintenance costs vary but small-scale hydro systems are usually very reliable.
- There may be various regulatory hurdles to overcome, including issues with the Environment Agency.

Biomass (biofuels)

Biomass is produced from organic materials, either directly from plants or indirectly from industrial, commercial, domestic or agricultural products. It is often called 'bioenergy' or 'biofuels'. It doesn't include fossil fuels, which have taken millions of years to be created.

How it works (biomass):

Biomass materials such as wood and leaves can be compacted into small pellet shapes. Naturally-occurring resins and binders such as lignin in the biomass hold wood pellets together, so they do not usually contain any additives. Woodchips are produced from various types of wood residue, manufacturing waste, and energy crops.

There are two main ways of using biomass to heat a domestic property:

- Stand-alone stoves provide space heating for a room. They can be fuelled by logs or pellets although only pellets are suitable for automatic feed. They are usually 6–12 kW in output, and some models can be fitted with a back boiler to provide water heating.
- Boilers connected to central heating and hot water systems. These can be fuelled by pellets, logs or chips, and are typically around 15kW. There are many such boilers available. Log boilers have to be loaded by hand and may be unsuitable for some situations. Automatic pellet and woodchip systems have a hopper which refuels the boiler at regular intervals but they can be more expensive.

Practicalities (biomass):

Fuel:

- Pellets and woodchips are purchased from a retailer and are available in large quantities, which make it more economical. Use a local fuel retailer to minimize transport miles to your home as well as supporting local employment (see **www.logpile.co.uk**).

- The moisture content of the biofuel is an important factor and the maximum moisture content will be dictated by the requirements of the boiler. If you are using wood, only seasoned wood should be used, which takes one to two years. Damp wood is heavier and provides less heat when burnt. Freshly felled wood ('green wood') may contain up to 50 per cent moisture, whereas 'dry' wood is specified as having a moisture content of 10–15 per cent.

- You will need storage space for the fuel and appropriate access to the boiler for loading. Wood should be stored outside with the top of the pile covered and the sides open to facilitate natural air drying.

- You can turn old newspapers into compact pulp logs with specially designed 'Logmaker' products (see various eco-product catalogues). One newspaper will produce one log, and each log will burn for up to an hour. Easy to use, this is an ideal use of newspaper if you're miles from recycling facilities.

Boiler:

- You will need a flue fitted for ventilation and it must be the correct specifications for the fuel you are using.

- Ensure your fire is getting sufficient air. A properly aerated fireplace benefits from providing more heat, less smoke and is more efficient.

- Chimneys should be swept at least twice a year.

General:

- Biomass is not so practical for the average urban household but if you are able to accommodate the equipment, biomass does have its benefits.

- Burning wood and waste is highly polluting without good filters or an advanced burner. The installation must comply with all safety and Building Regulations. Under the Clean Air Act, wood can only be burnt in exempted appliances.

- If the building is listed or in an area of outstanding natural beauty (AONB), then you will need to check with your Local Authority Planning Department before a flue is fitted.

Cost savings

PLEASE NOTE: Use this table in conjunction with notes following it – there are many assumptions!

table 5.1 financial and environmental savings (microgeneration)

Form of Microgeneration	Typical Cost (incl. grants) (£)	Annual financial savings (£)	Payback (yrs)	Lifespan of equipment (yrs)	Lifetime savings (£)	Annual CO_2 savings (tonnes)	Lifetime CO_2 savings (tonnes)	£ spent/ tonne CO_2 saved
Solar hot water (4m²)	3,700	40	92	20	807	338	7	557
Photovoltaics (2.5kWp)	13,000	215	61	25	5,368	1,138	28	464
Photovoltaics (2.5kWp) + ROCs	13,000	408	32	25	10,199	1,138	28	464
Microwind – roof-mounted (1kW)	1,329	30	44	10	302	160	2	844
Small wind – mast-mounted (5–6kW) + ROCs	17,500	850	21	25	21,256	2,372	58	300
Ground source heat pump (typical 6–8kW system) – off the gas grid	12,800	885	14.5	20	17,691	4,688	92	139

Ground source heat pump (typical 6–8kW system) – on the gas grid	IT IS VERY DIFFICULT TO JUSTIFY THIS TECHNOLOGY WHEN GAS IS AVAILABLE – See notes below							
Hydro power – a typical 5kW domestic scheme	20– up to 2,500)	25,000 (Grants	SITE SPECIFIC – GET PROFESSIONAL ADVICE					
Biofuels (stand-alone heater)	3,000 (Grants up to 600)		HIGHLY VARIABLE – See notes below					
Biofuels (pellet boiler) – 15kW	6,750	n/a	n/a	n/a	15	n/a	4,460	66	103

Notes:

General

- **PLEASE NOTE:** All the above figures are subject to great variability due to: wide price variation of products and associated installation; performance for many systems being very sensitive to location and weather; and difficulty in assessing realistic lifespans. Bear in mind some systems may require significant maintenance costs. PLEASE USE FIGURES ONLY AS A GUIDE – IT IS RECOMMENDED THAT YOU OBTAIN SPECIALIST ADVICE BEFORE INSTALLING ANY MICROGENERATION SYSTEM.

- **Fuel prices** and **Carbon intensity:**
  - Assume $0.21kgCO_2$/kWh for gas consumption at a cost of 2.51p/kWh.
  - Assume $0.53kgCO_2$/kWh for electricity consumption at a cost of 10p/kWh.

- **Net-metering** – If you produce excess energy (wind, photovoltaic and hydro) it maybe possible to export this via a net meter and receive some value for the energy. However, this may be significantly lower per unit than you are paying for imported electricity and there could be a cost of about £100 to set up.

- **ROCs** – It is more likely that larger systems will be able to set up ROC payment systems, in particular wind and photovoltaics. You will need a specific type of meter to do this. However, payments for ROC 'equivalents' have recently been increased by at least one company (Good Energy) and so this could be a very important factor in your financial calculations. In some countries, such as Germany, they pay small generators as much as three times electricity prices as an incentive.

Solar hot water

- Costs typically vary between £3,200 and £4,500, average £4,100 (source: Energy Saving Trust). Grants of up to £400 currently available. Evacuated tube systems are more advanced in design than flat plate, and so can be more expensive.

- Savings of 350–400kg of carbon dioxide emissions per year are likely (source: Energy Saving Trust). However, a usability fraction of 90 per cent has been assumed as homes are not usually occupied 365 days a year and even if they were, perhaps not all of the energy in the solar hot water would be used.

- Most systems need some electricity to run pumps ('parasitic energy') which would reduce the financial and environmental savings shown.
- Assumes house is currently on mains gas. Savings would be greater if replacing an electric hot water system.
- Lifespan of 20 years is likely to be a minimum for most parts, but the pump will probably need replacing earlier.

Photovoltaics

- The size of the system is dictated by the amount of electricity required. Most domestic systems are around 2.5kWp.
- Costs typically vary between £10,000 and £18,000, average £15,500 (source: Energy Saving Trust). Prices for PV systems vary depending on the size of the system to be installed, type of PV cell used and the nature of the actual building on which the PV is mounted.
- For these calculations the cost has been discounted by the current maximum Government grant of £2,500.
- Solar tiles cost more than conventional panels and panels that are integrated into a roof are more expensive than those that sit on top.
- Each kWp can save approximately 455kg of carbon dioxide emissions per year (source: Energy Saving Trust).
- Assume excess electricity exported and sold to grid (usually about 50 per cent) using net-metering.

Photovoltaics (+ROCs)

- Assume ROCs income of 9p/kWh (Good Energy, Oct 2007).

Microwind (1kW)

- At the moment there is not enough data from existing wind turbine installations to provide an accurate figure of how much energy and carbon could typically be saved – *so take care in using this data.*
- Figures used in this table for CO_2 emission savings were based on an on line tool that estimated the output of a 'Windsave' 1kW wind turbine (see **www.warwickwindtrials.org.uk**) using a wind speed of 5m/s (this is very good for an urban location).
- Costs based on 'Windsave' 1kW wind turbine purchased from B&Q (October 2007) less 30 per cent Government

grant. There may be additional planning permission costs of up to £135. It is also assumed that there are no additional building costs to reinforce building to install turbine.

- Lifespan from Windsave Ltd – 'expected safe life' of ten years.
- Assume excess electricity exported to grid and householder on net-metering (this may not be possible in many cases).

Small wind (5–6kW)

- For mast-mounted wind turbines, the costs are inclusive of the turbine, mast, inverters, battery storage (if required) and installation. However, it's important to remember that costs always vary depending on location and the size and type of system.
- Assume current maximum Government grant of £2,500.
- Assume ROCs income of 9p/kWh (Good Energy, Oct 2007).
- Performance based on actual data over four years from HHP averaged two different 6kW models (for further information, see www.hockertonhousingproject.org.uk).

Ground source heat pumps

- This type of microgeneration does have a cost to run! You need to take into account the energy required to run the system when it is installed – the Coefficient of performance (CoP) is the ratio of units of heat/hot water produced by a heat pump, for each unit of electricity used to drive the compressor and pump. A typical CoP is 3.5, which has been used in these calculations.
- For a property not on gas grid, assume substituting typical heating energy requirements of approx. 12,000kWh.
- Costs vary between £7,300 and £11,800, typically £10,000 (not including price of distribution system) for a 6–8kW system (source: Energy Saving Trust). For these calculations £10,000 is used plus £4,000 for distribution system less the current maximum Government grant of £1,200.
- A ground source heat pump can have lower running costs than oil, LPG, coal and electric heating systems. However, it is more expensive than mains gas. It is most likely to be an option where there is no access to natural gas. This is because you need to use 1 unit of electricity to gain 3.5 units of useful delivered energy (e.g. hot water), and since electricity is currently nearly four times the price of gas, the electricity costs will almost cancel out gas cost savings!

- If a 'geen' electricity tariff supplied the electricity for the pump, the carbon dioxide emissions could be reduced to zero. You could also run the pump using secondary microgeneration, such as wind or solar.

Hydro power

- Hydro costs are very site-specific and are related to energy output. For low head systems (assuming there is an existing pond or weir), costs may be in the region of £4,000 per kW installed up to about 10kW and would drop per kW for larger schemes. For medium heads, there is a fixed cost of about £10,000 and then about £2,500 per kW up to around 10kW – unit costs drop for larger schemes (source: Energy Saving Trust).

Biomass/biofuels

- Costs for a 15kW pellet boiler are typically about £8,000 and there are Government grants of up to £1,500.
- Savings will depend on how much they are used and which fuel you are replacing. Unlike other forms of renewable energy, biomass systems require you to pay for the fuel. Fuel costs generally depend on the distance from your supplier and whether you can buy in large quantities. In general fuel costs of pellets are comparable with gas and so there would be no real financial savings. Using your own supply of logs could provide significant cost savings over gas, depending on whether it is your own wood and how much you are willing to get involved with collection and storage. Future price rises of gas or electricity would make this a more attractive option financially.
- If you use biofuels as an alternative to electric heating systems, then the financial savings would compare very favourably with those of a ground source heat pump shown in the table.
- Although financial savings are not shown for the reasons above, there are very definite environmental savings, based on substituting fossil fuel use. In these calculations it has been assumed that biofuels replace the typical gas required for a three-bed semi-detached home for heating and hot water.

06

energy saving in the garden

In this chapter you will learn:
- what can be done to reduce energy use in the garden
- why patio heaters are bad for the environment
- about other good environmental practice in the garden.

Gardening can benefit the environment, for example, by creating spaces for wildlife or producing food which has not had to travel long distances. However, some things we do in the garden are not so good for the environment. We increasingly use our gardens as extensions of the house, where we can enjoy being outdoors for longer without discomfort. This has resulted in a dramatic increase in equipment to support this desire, including sophisticated outdoor lighting, water pumps, patio heaters, hot tubs, and heated swimming pools. Much of this equipment uses large amounts of energy and energy-efficiency is often low on the product's selling points.

So how can we ensure that the garden space does not become a terrible drain on our pockets with high energy costs and an environmental blot on the landscape?

No cost actions

- **Put on a jumper** – When it starts to cool down outside, put on additional layers of clothing rather than using an outdoor heater. Wrapping up warm or going indoors when you get chilly is a much greener option. Outdoor heaters that are powered by gas or electricity use a lot of energy and, therefore, contribute to climate change. It has been estimated that the average patio heater emits about the same amount of carbon dioxide (CO_2) in four hours as the average car emits in a whole day.

Patio heaters warm gardens and the earth!

A recent survey by British Gas suggests that, following the introduction of the smoking ban this summer, there could be a massive increase in the use of patio heaters. The survey found that half of all pubs in Scotland bought one or more patio heaters after the smoking ban was imposed there in March 2006. English pubs are expected to follow suit with an estimated minimum of 40,000 additional heaters being purchased. In addition, the Energy Saving Trust predicts that the number of patio heaters owned by households in the UK will increase from an approximate 1.2 million in 2007 to 2.3 million in 2008.

What was once considered a smart, 'must-have' appliance as the UK moved towards a more continental style of dining, is now seen as environmentally destructive. Although estimates of the impact

---

that patio heaters have on climate change vary, it is generally agreed that they are damaging. Some calculations show that a single heater releases more CO_2 into the atmosphere each year than the average fuel-hungry 4x4 car. British Gas estimates that the additional heaters bought by English pubs in response to the smoking ban could be responsible for generating between 160,000 and 320,000 tonnes of carbon.

This damaging effect has led to a call from environmental campaigners Friends of the Earth for the Government to ban the sale of patio heaters. Some retailers, such as Wyevale Garden Centres, Notcutts Garden Centres and Marks & Spencer have already taken the initiative and have stopped stocking them. The Energy Saving Trust (EST) and the Mayor of London, Ken Livingstone, have urged other retailers to follow this lead.

Spokesman for the EST, Jon McGowan says 'It just seems absolutely daft and a bad use of our resource that we have these heaters which heat the outside air rather than us putting on a jumper, getting a blanket or putting a wrap around us when we're outside in the summer. In some ways patio heaters are taking our desire for luxury and our desire to defeat the elements to quite a ridiculous degree.'

- **Share appliances** – How often do you really use that garden shredder or circular saw? Save money and save the energy needed to manufacture more appliances by sharing gardening equipment. Sharing can be quite formal, such as setting up a tool library/bank within a community or with neighbours, or through very informal arrangements with neighbours. You will also benefit by not having to take up so much space in the house, garden or shed to store infrequently-used equipment. Of course you may also discover hidden professional/DIY talents of your own or neighbours that can also be shared.

- **Saving water use** – In hot, dry weather water used outdoors can account for up to half of domestic use. Saving water saves energy, and if you are on a meter, this also saves you money. Indeed if you use a sprinkler, your water company may insist that you have a meter fitted (they can use as much water in an hour as a family of four uses in a day!) Significant energy is used to treat, purify (to drinking standard) and pump water to our homes. Here are some ideas for saving water:

- Use a watering can instead of a hose pipe.
- If you do use a hose, control the flow by using a trigger.
- Only use a rose on your watering can when watering young seedlings. For other plants the water should be aimed at the roots where it is needed.
- Water during cooler parts of the day, such as early in the morning or late at night, to prevent water evaporating before it reaches the roots.
- Watering plants too often will encourage them to develop shallow roots and weaken them.
- Young plants and seedlings need more water, whilst more established plants can survive for longer without water.
- Longer grass helps keep moisture in the soil.
- Water thoroughly but less often rather than frequent 'sprinkling' as this will encourage roots to find water deeper in the ground.
- Choose grass varieties that are suited to dry conditions like fescue grass or smooth-stalked meadow so that you do not have to water your lawn as often.
- **Make use of greywater in the garden** – Cooled water from your shower, sink and laundry can all be re-used to water non-edible plants in the garden but avoid applying it directly on to foliage.

Low cost actions

Cut out greenhouse heating

Heating a greenhouse over the winter uses energy, costs you money and contributes to climate change. By thinking carefully when erecting and using your greenhouse, you could avoid the need for winter heating:

- Choose a sunny, un-shaded position for your greenhouse that benefits from sun all day.
- A lean-to greenhouse erected against a house wall will need less heating.
- A part-brick or part-timber greenhouse will conserve heat better than all-glass varieties.
- Heat will be lost from poorly-fitting glass panes and doors so seal any gaps.

- Dirty glass in your greenhouse will dramatically reduce light levels and heating so keep it clean.
- Instead of storing less hardy plants in the greenhouse, move them indoors for the winter.

Get a water butt

Almost 100,000 litres of water falls on the average UK rooftop every year so you can easily save on mains water by collecting rainwater to use on your garden. If you are on a water meter then you will also save money.

A few things to consider when considering installing a water butt:

- Use a lid to stop leaves collecting and to prevent small animals and birds from falling in and drowning.
- Connector kits are available that allow you to link up two or more water butts so you are not restricted to only collecting enough water for one butt.
- You may be able to purchase a water butt from your water company or council at a subsidized price.

Compost garden and kitchen waste

At least one third of the waste from our homes is kitchen or garden waste that can be composted. A compost heap or a compost bin will convert this waste into valuable compost which can be used on the garden to condition the soil and fertilize and mulch your plants. If you do not have a garden yourself, consider an allotment or offer your organic waste to a neighbour who could make use of it. Otherwise, your local council will be able to tell you how to dispose of your kitchen and garden waste.

Why compost?
- Saves money by reducing your need to buy artificial fertilizers.
- Reduces energy and pollution from artificial fertilizers – A large amount of energy is used to produce artificial fertilizers so substituting home-produced compost will save energy. Nitrogen-fertilizers also generate nitrous oxide, another greenhouse gas which can contaminate soil and water and get into the food chain.

- Reduces pollution from waste methane – Organic material such as kitchen and garden waste will create methane when deposited in landfill sites. Methane is another greenhouse gas and is more than 20 times as damaging as CO_2.
- Reduces demand for commercially extracted peat-based compost which is taken from important natural wildlife sites.

Practicalities (composting):

- You can compost all garden waste such as grass cuttings, prunings, leaves, hedge trimmings.
- You can compost most of your kitchen/household 'organic' waste such as fruit and vegetable scraps, tea bags, coffee grounds, egg shells, small amounts of shredded paper and soft cardboard, animal hair and even vacuum dust (only from woollen carpets).
- You should avoid composting meat, cheeses, fish, cooked food, disposable nappies, cat or dog excrement.
- If you are unsure about any aspect of home composting there is plenty of advice available. RecycleNow have a guide to home composting and also run a helpline: call 0845 600 0323 or see **www.recyclenow.com/home_composting**. Local authorities also usually offer advice.
- You can buy compost bins from your local garden centre or DIY store. Many councils also sell them, often at a reduced cost, and subsidized compost bins are available via RecycleNow (**www.recyclenow.com/home_composting**) who have distributed over a million around the UK.
- Many councils now collect garden waste via a 'green bag' scheme. Collections are usually free, but some councils may charge a small fee.

Other low cost actions

- **Use less mowing energy** – A petrol or diesel mower can cause more pollution than several cars! Use an electric mower, or even better, a manual mower instead. Reducing the grassed area of your garden will reduce the amount of energy you use for mowing. You could include larger areas of rockery, flowerbeds, wild areas or a vegetable patch.
- **Plan a water-efficient garden** – A healthy soil with good compost content will retain moisture and nutrients and choosing drought-tolerant plants will mean less watering. Planting shrubs and trees through matting or using mulches,

such as wood bark, around established plants will help to retain moisture and control weeds.
- **Use infrared** – If you have exterior lights, fit infrared sensors so that the lights only come on when you pass in front of them.

Investment actions

Grow your own organic food

Growing at least some of your own food can be very rewarding for you and the environment. It is also a great way of keeping fit!

Why grow your own?

- Gives you the personal satisfaction of growing your own fresh produce.
- Reduces the amount you spend on organic fruit and vegetables.
- Reduces the environmental impact caused by the production, packaging and transportation of food grown commercially.
- Reduces the use of pesticides which are harmful to people, wildlife and the environment.
- Improves your health – Save money on that gym membership and use your energy to do something useful! Your own home-grown organic produce, freshly harvested and prepared, is also likely to be a lot more nutritious than food from the supermarket which has been transported many miles and stored.
- Re-connects us with the earth and nature, something which is increasingly recognized as being important for our sense of well-being.

> If all food was sourced from 12 miles of where it is eaten, environmental and congestion costs would be reduced by 90 per cent. (Source: **www.eastsideclimateaction.org.uk**)

Practicalities (grow your own food):

- Even the smallest space can be used as a garden. Local allotments offer larger areas for cultivation and if they are shared between friends they can also provide a social experience.

- Gardening can be enjoyed by anyone – there are no age restrictions.
- Use pesticides responsibly and only as a last resort. Try to work with nature to control pests and weeds instead.

Plant trees and bushes

Trees, shrubs and hedges are useful additions to your garden if you have the space to include some. They provide:

- a windbreak to shelter colder aspects of your house, thereby saving on energy used for heating. (more information see Chapter 04)
- shading for those parts of your house which can get too hot (for more information see Chapter 04)
- a valuable habitat for wildlife
- absorption of CO_2 (which fences and walls do not!).

Take care not to plant trees too near to buildings though, as their root systems can cause structural damage. Also, choose indigenous varieties rather than non-native species.

Other environmental actions

- **Avoid peat-based products** – Buy peat-free compost, mulches, soil improvers and fertilizers – they are just as good and help to protect precious peat bogs.
- **Encourage wildlife** – Create a variety of habitats and provide sources of food to encourage animals and insects into your garden. For example, flowering plants will attract bees, butterflies and other insects, and trees and shrubs that produce berries will provide food for birds. Bird tables and nest boxes will also encourage a variety of birds into your garden.
- **Build a pond** – Ponds are simple to make and provide a haven for frogs, toads, newts, dragonflies and other insects.
- **Plant wildflowers** – Not only will this provide a haven for wildlife but it can help to re-establish rare wild plants. Obtain information about sources of wildflower plants/seeds from your local branch of the British Trust for Conservation Volunteers or other wildlife organization.

- **Choose sustainable wood products** – Ensure that timber and wood products such as garden sheds and furniture have been produced sustainably. They should carry the Forest Stewardship Council (FSC) or Programme for the Endorsement of Forest Certification Schemes (PEFC) label.

- **Reclaim and recycle** – Wherever possible, buy decking, planters and garden ornaments which have been made from reclaimed or recycled materials. You could even make things yourself from old timber, metal and plastic containers.

- **Choose sustainable charcoal** – Make sure the charcoal you use for your barbecue has been produced sustainably; it should carry the FSC, PEFC or other forest certification scheme label. Shockingly, only a small percentage of the charcoal used on our barbecues is actually made in the UK. Charcoal is often imported from thousands of miles away, resulting in a great deal of energy being used for transportation. Buying sustainable, locally-produced charcoal helps prevent global deforestation and illegal logging.

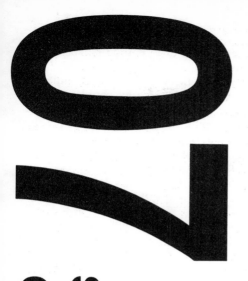

07

saving energy on the road

In this chapter you will learn:
- how to drive and use less fuel
- how to find out about fuel efficiencies of different cars
- what the alternatives are to petrol and diesel cars
- options for car sharing.

Introduction

The type of car you own, the way you drive it and the type of fuel you use can have a big impact on its running costs and the emissions it produces. Motoring is one of the biggest expenditures in most households and driving more carefully could save you hundreds of pounds a year in petrol or diesel. With fuel prices rising all the time, this could become an even bigger saving in the future. Adopting a fuel-saving driving style is easy, and once this becomes the norm, not only will you start to make real financial savings, but you'll also be doing your bit for the environment. Personal car travel is responsible for 13 per cent of the UK's total greenhouse gas emissions and this is forecast to rise in the future; in the past 30 years, traffic on our roads has more than doubled and the UK is now one of the most car-dependent countries in Europe. With most road journeys made in the UK being less than five miles, a large proportion of driving is done with a relatively cold engine and, therefore, at the lowest efficiency. Car use can provide convenience, but at what cost to the environment, our pocket and people's long-term health?

No cost actions

There are a number of actions, many quite small, that you can take to reduce the amount of fuel you burn and so cut down on CO_2 emissions. The suggestions below have been grouped by how much effort they require. Clearly, different people will find some actions easier than others, in part due to their current approach to driving – changing habits is often harder than buying solutions.

> ### Eco-driving test!
>
> In September 2007 a new section to the driving theory test was introduced by the Driving Standards Agency. You are required to know more about fuel-efficient driving. The aim is to cut down on carbon emissions and save fuel at the same time.

Easy to do

- **Slow down** – For the optimum fuel economy, drive at a steady speed between 40–50mph (but check your vehicle manual as this varies from model to model). Driving at 50mph can use up to 25 per cent less fuel than at 70mph. Also bear in mind:
  - when you are driving on motorways, stick to the speed limit – as well as being legal and a safer speed, you will save money.
  - driving at slower speeds is less intimidating for cyclists and pedestrians and, should an accident occur, the higher the speed, the greater will be the severity of injuries.

- **Be smooth** – Avoid sharp braking and accelerating, particularly as you approach traffic lights, junctions and roundabouts. According to the RAC, this style of driving can save as much as 30 per cent on fuel costs, reduce wear and tear on the vehicle and result in a more pleasant journey.

- **Limit air conditioning** – it increases fuel consumption by about 10 per cent – try to alternate it with using your air vents on hot days.

- **Limit use of on-board electrical devices** (like mobile phone chargers) – only use them when necessary as they also increase fuel consumption.

- **Do not let the engine run to warm up when starting from cold** – Idling to heat the engine wastes fuel and causes rapid engine wear.

- **Switch off the engine** if you are stationary for more than two minutes – idling for this long burns more fuel than it takes to restart the engine (source: Environmental Transport Association).

- **Do not open the windows** unless you really need to – Opening windows increases wind resistance and so reduces efficiency.

Some effort

- **Avoid driving too close to the car in front** – This is not only risky and dangerous it makes it harder to drive smoothly and therefore efficiently.

- **Change gear at the right time** – As a general rule, shift up a gear at 2500rpm for petrol cars and 2000rpm for diesel cars.

- **Use the 'cruise control' setting on long journeys,** if you have one – This will help you to drive more smoothly and save fuel.
- **Keep your car tyres properly inflated** – Under inflated tyres create more resistance when your car is moving which means your engine has to work harder, more fuel is used and more CO_2 emissions are produced. Simply check and adjust your tyre pressures regularly and particularly before long journeys or significant changes to your normal loads (number of passengers and luggage). This will also help to increase the life of your tyres. Check your car manual for the correct tyre pressures under different circumstances (including time of year) and take care not to over-inflate tyres as well, as this can make your car less safe.
- **Remove clutter from your boot** – It is extra weight that your engine has to lug around and by simply removing it you could reduce your engine's workload and hence save fuel.
- **Remove roof boxes when they are not in use** – Accessories such as roof racks, bike carriers, and roof boxes increase the air resistance of your car and hence reduce its fuel efficiency.

More effort

- **Plan your journeys** to avoid congestion, road works and getting lost – These factors prevent you from driving smoothly and efficiently. It may seem odd, but according to the RAC, using the new M6 toll road, for example, which is free from congestion and has a much better surface, could actually save you money.
- **Avoid short car journeys** – A cold engine uses almost twice as much fuel as a warmer one and catalytic converters can take five miles to become effective. Identify those journeys which you could make on foot, by bike or using public transport. It will be good for your health, your pocket, and the environment. Transport Direct have public transport information: **www.transportdirect.org.uk**. The national cyclists' organization (CTC) has details of cycle routes in your area: **www.ctc.org.uk**.
- **Share the 'school run'** – Sharing with other parents is a great way to cut congestion, reduce emissions and save on your fuel bill. Liftshare Ltd helps you find other parents with whom to share the school run (**www.school-run.org**) or, alternatively, contact your child's school to ask them to look into a scheme.

Sustrans, the sustainable transport charity, also provides more information about school travel plans: www.saferoutestoschools.org.uk/.

- **Avoid city driving** – City driving consumes far more fuel per mile than motorway or other out-of-town driving. Many cities provide 'Park-and-Ride' schemes which are convenient and avoid costly parking fees.

Low cost actions

Car maintenance

Keep your car in peak running condition – Maintaining your vehicle helps to ensure that it is fuel-efficient and less polluting. Consult your car manual paying particular attention to environmental issues. These are now considered far more regularly by car manufacturers. Factors such as steering alignment and tracking can affect fuel efficiency so it pays to have these checked regularly. Dirty air filters can seriously reduce your fuel economy. They could also mean you would fail a roadside emissions test. Change them as soon as they get dirty.

Why not teach yourself basic car mechanics and bicycle repair skills? Try **www.sustrans.org.uk/webfiles/travelsmart/maintenance.pdf**.

Join or organize a car share/car club

Perhaps surprisingly, most cars are actually parked for over 90 per cent of their lives. It might therefore be worth considering how much you actually need to own a car and whether there are more cost effective options, such as car sharing. Not surprisingly with increasing costs to run cars and increasing congestion, car-sharing schemes are becoming more popular than ever. Car-sharing lanes are even being introduced on some of the worse affected roads. The benefits of car sharing include:

- reduced travel costs for each person
- reduced traffic resulting in improved air quality and less carbon emissions
- less congestion on the roads, reducing time spent commuting
- increased chance of finding a parking space
- improvment in road safety.

Finding or creating a car sharing scheme

- Informal car sharing can easily be arranged with friends, family, colleagues and close neighbours. It could involve simply sharing lifts to work, school and the shops.

- Sharing ownership of a car is more complex, but perfectly feasible if you have similar journeys and needs for transport.

- There are a number of organized schemes available via the internet. There are others that are specifically organized for people in certain organizations or businesses. You can check your local council website for organized schemes in your area or look up Carplus (**www.carplus.org.uk**).

- Car clubs allow members to 'hire' a vehicle. Vehicles are parked in reserved parking spaces, near to homes or workplaces, and can be used and paid for on an hourly, daily or weekly basis. It might just make your life a lot simpler.

Share lifts and save pounds

Liftshare Ltd, operators of the UK's largest car share network (**www.liftshare.com**) are facilitating National Liftshare Day. This annual event takes place on the 14 June and seeks to raise awareness of the benefits of car sharing. Liftshare Ltd calculates that a typical car sharer will save themselves approximately £1,000 and 1 tonne of CO_2 each year by sharing their daily journey!

In 2005, over 60 per cent of cars on the road had only one occupant and 85 per cent of commuters travelled alone by car. Just a 2 per cent rise in occupancy would result in a reduction of five billion kilometres of road travel.

Registering with Liftshare Ltd is free and only takes a few minutes. There are already more than 169,000 registered car sharers around the UK contributing to an estimated saving of more than 12,000 tonnes of CO_2 emissions each year.

Further information about the National Liftshare Day can be found at **www.nationalliftshareday.org**.

Car-sharing lanes

Car-sharing lanes have been set up in areas of the UK that experience high congestion levels to bias cars that have more than one occupant. There are such schemes running currently in Leeds and Gloucestershire and there are plans to build two more, one on the M606 and M62, and another on the M1.

To ensure that drivers do not abuse these traffic control measures, cameras may be used to check occupancy levels in cars, and drivers who use the lanes incorrectly will be prosecuted.

Other actions

- **Switch to energy-saving tyres** – Michelin have produced a special tyre which they claim is 20 per cent freer rolling over a conventional design and can save 6 per cent in fuel use over 12,000 miles.
- **Rent a car** on a pay-as-you-drive scheme rather than buying one. Smartmoves has a growing list of pay-as-you-drive car clubs: **www.smartmoves.co.uk.**
- **Change to low viscosity motor oil** – It lubricates the moving parts of the engine better than ordinary oils, reducing friction and hence fuel consumption and CO_2 emissions.

Investment actions

Change to less polluting fuels

As well as the environmental benefits, electric and hybrid cars may benefit from reduced or exempt congestion charges (e.g. London), worth up to £2,000. You can also park for free in Manchester.

- **Biofuels** (biodiesel and bioethanol) – Biofuels are produced from crops such as oil seed rape or sugar beet, and burning them produces lower emissions of greenhouse gases. Many cars can use biofuels with little or no modification to the engine. Biofuels are mixed with either petrol or diesel and all cars can run on petrol/diesel with up to 5 per cent biofuel blended in. Cars that can run on an 85 per cent blend of bioethanol (known as E85) are also available. There are 150 filling stations in the UK that supply biofuel and the number is growing. See **www.biodieselfillingstations.co.uk.** Alternatively, you can go on courses to find out how to make your own – see **www.lowimpact.org** (but don't forget to pay the tax!).
- **Electric cars** do not produce any emissions when you drive them but emissions are produced when the electricity is generated to charge the batteries (unless of course you charge

it from a renewable energy source). These cars benefit from zero or much lower congestion charges.

- **Hybrid cars** use a petrol engine in combination with a battery and are therefore very fuel efficient without any compromise on performance. The Toyota Prius is the best known model available in the UK, having benefited in recent years from rising fuel prices. These cars also benefit from reduced congestion charges.

- **Liquid petroleum gas** (LPG) cars cannot be purchased new in the UK, but petrol cars can be converted to run on LPG. If you are converting an older petrol car there will be an additional benefit of a reduction in air quality pollutants. The conversion needs to be well engineered and maintained.

Change to a fuel-efficient car

If you definitely need to own a car, then run the smallest most fuel-efficient vehicle you think is practically sensible. With a budget of about £10,000, purchasing a fuel-efficient car could save you over £10 a week, as well as attracting lower Vehicle Excise Duty. Diesel cars tend to be more fuel-efficient and produce less CO_2, but they can produce more pollutants that affect air quality, aggravating asthma and other respiratory conditions.

Practicalities (finding a fuel-efficient car):

- As a general rule, the smaller the car and engine, the better the fuel efficiency.

- Buying a more fuel-efficient car doesn't mean you have to compromise necessarily on quality and style. It might just be a matter of carefully choosing a more efficient version of a fairly standard model range.

- Check the fuel economy label (see Figure 7.1).

- Manufacturers are required to include fuel consumption and CO_2 emissions data in all brochures and printed advertisements.

- There are several resources you can use to find a specific fuel-efficient car:

    - **Car Fuel Database** of the Vehicle Certification Agency **www.vcacarfueldata.org.uk** – You can search by fuel economy, tax band and car make or model.

- Best on CO_2 (www.dft.gov.uk/ActOnCO2) – A new website (2007) by the Department of Transport to help people choose the most environmentally-friendly vehicle. The site uses a ranking system devised with 'What Car?' magazine to find out which top ten new cars have the lowest CO_2 in their class.
- Environmental Transport Association (www.eta.co.uk) – Have a 'Car Buyer's Guide' showing the environmental rating of all new cars on the market.

Fuel economy label (see Figure 7.1)

Car showrooms have fuel economy labels, similar to the energy efficiency labels that appear on many household appliances, which show you how fuel efficient each new car is. The labels show:

- rating from band A to G, with band A being the most fuel efficient
- level of CO_2 emissions – lower CO_2 emissions mean lower Vehicle Tax, lower running costs and less environmental impact
- estimated fuel costs for 12,000 miles of driving
- Vehicle Tax for 12 months
- fuel consumption figures expressed both in litres per 100 kilometres (l/100km) and in miles per gallon (mpg). Figures are given for urban, extra-urban and combined conditions separately.

Fuel Economy

CO₂ emission figure (g/km)

<100	A
101-120	B
121-150	C
151-165	D
166-185	E
186-225	F
226+	G

◄ C   130 g/km

Fuel cost (estimated) for 12,000 miles
A fuel cost figure indicates to the consumer a guide fuel price for comparison purposes. This figure is
calculated by using the combined drive cycle (town centre and motorway) and average fuel price.
Re-calculated annually, the current cost per litre is as follows – petrol 87p, diesel 93p and LPG 46p
(VCA May 2007)

VED for 12 months
Vehicle excise duty (VED) or road tax varies according to the CO₂ emissions and fuel type of the vehicle.

Environmental Information

A guide on fuel economy and CO₂ emissions which contains data for all new passenger car models is
available at any point of sale free of charge. In addition to the fuel efficiency of a car, driving behaviour
as well as other non-technical factors play a role in determining a car's fuel consumption and CO₂
emissions. CO₂ is the main greenhouse gas responsible for global warming.

Make/Model:	Engine Capacity (cc):
Fuel Type:	Transmission:

Fuel Consumption:

Drive cycle	Litres/100km	Mpg
Urban		
Extra-urban		
Combined		

Carbon dioxide emissions (g/km):
Important note: Some specifications of this make/model may have lower CO₂ emissions than this.
Check with your dealer.

THE MOTOR INDUSTRY SMMT   LowC^VP low carbon vehicle partnership   Department for Transport   VCA

figure 7.1 fuel economy label (reproduced with the kind permission of VCA)

table 7.1 examples of the impact of driving behaviour on fuel consumption of cars

Measure	Impact on fuel consumption	Annual CO_2 savings (kg)	Notes
Make sure you have correct tyre pressure	Increases by 5 per cent if tyre pressure is down 0.5 bar	140[1]	Assumes the average driving distance of a European car at 14,000km
Apply smart driving (Eco-driving)	12 per cent	200[1]	Plan your journey, start your car moving without pressing down the throttle, shift to a higher gear as soon as possible (at 2,000–2,500rpm), keep the speed steady and look ahead to avoid sudden breaking and accelerating. Turn off the engine even at short stops!
Reduce your speed from 110km per hour to 90km per hour for 10 per cent of your driving distance	Decreased by 20 per cent	35[1]	Assumes the average driving distance of a European car at 14,000km
Replace your short car journeys with biking		240[1]	Avoid (e.g. your trip to work back and forth) 6km during 200 days per year and that you drive an average new car in 2003

Consider the fuel economy, when replacing your old car with a new one		660[1]	Assumes the average driving distance of a European car at 14,000km and that you choose a model that is 15 per cent less fuel consuming than an average new car in 2003

Note: [1]Source: Produced by European Commission carbon calculator – see **www.mycarbonfootprint.eu** for more details about assumptions used to determine CO_2 emission reductions.

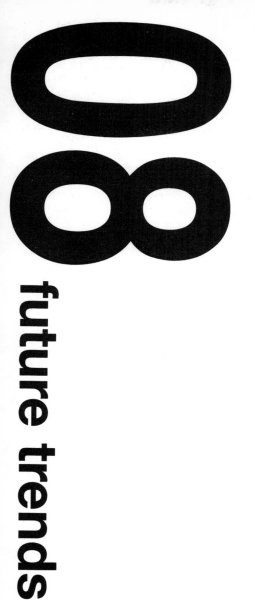

08

future trends

In this chapter you will learn:
- about possible changes to our lifestyles in a low carbon future.

General trends

With environmental issues of growing importance, politicians are increasingly embracing ways of addressing them. There are now legally agreed and binding targets at a broader level, across the EU and worldwide, as it is recognized that climate change has no borders. It is therefore no surprise that governments are looking for the easiest ways of reducing greenhouse gas emissions and, with the housing sector accounting for over a quarter of the UK's CO_2 emissions, the domestic consumer is inevitably going to become a growing target for action.

Home energy audits

The recent introduction of Home Information Packs, which includes a requirement for an energy efficiency assessment (Energy Performance Certificate – see Chapter 02) will clearly improve homebuyers' awareness and understanding of energy issues in their home, and encourage more action to reduce energy use. It is likely, however, that home energy audits will be extended in the future to all homeowners, irrespective of whether the house is being sold. Energy companies will no doubt be encouraged/coerced to play a role in this as they are nudged toward becoming energy service companies rather than simply energy suppliers. This could include any of the following:

- Energy companies to check customers' meters at least twice a year and put more information on their bills to allow them to compare their energy use and CO_2 impact over time.
- Energy suppliers to deliver smart meters (see Chapter 02) to all homes within the next decade and to offer real-time displays to all consumers who want them within the next three years. (Energy White Paper, May 2007.)
- Every UK home given an energy audit.
- Committing householders to make recommended changes – this is most likely to be a voluntary written statement initially.

Personal carbon allowances

The Government is looking into the feasibility of tradable personal carbon allowances. This would involve everyone being given a limited allowance of CO_2 emissions – a bit like a credit card, but adopting carbon as the currency.

It would work by first setting an overall emissions cap, and then emissions rights divided equally across the population. These 'carbon credits' are then surrendered upon the purchase of energy/fuel/transport. Those who need or want to emit more than their allowance will have to buy allowances from those who can emit less than their allowance. Over time, the overall emissions cap (and hence individual allocations) could be reduced in line with international or nationally adopted agreements.

The following carbon targets will give you an idea of how significant reduction requirements may be:

- World average CO_2 consumption: 3.8 tonnes per person.
- UK average CO_2 total per person in 2005: 10.4 tonnes.
- UKGovernment target for 2010: 8.32 tonnes.
- UK Government target for 2050: 4.16 tonnes.

More information can be found in a report by the Centre for Sustainable Energy (CSE) who were asked to research the issues – *A Rough Guide to Individual Carbon Trading – The ideas, the issues and the next steps* (published by Defra). It looks at whether personal carbon allowances could transform the carbon-emitting behaviour of people in the UK. (See **http://www.cse.org.uk/pdf/news1270.pdf** to view the report.)

Carbon reduction label

(Source: Carbon Trust website **www.carbontrust.co.uk**.)

As consumers we are familiar with labels on products giving us information, such as, where it was made, the ingredients, how many calories there are, etc. In the future we will also get information about the carbon content associated with the production of products to help differentiate between competing brands and enable us to make more informed decisions about relative environmental impacts. It will also hopefully encourage companies through this competition to find ways of making ongoing carbon reductions. Research undertaken by the Carbon Trust shows that 66 per cent of consumers say they want to know the carbon footprint of the products they buy.

Such a carbon reduction label is currently being trialled by a number of major brands including Walkers and Boots, in order to test and build consumer understanding. The first product to appear on shelves with the new logo was Walkers Cheese and Onion crisps – the company's best-selling flavour. Boots will be introducing point of sale material with the label to accompany the launch of Botanics and Ingredients range shampoos with a reduced carbon footprint. They will also be giving advice to consumers on how they can reduce their personal carbon footprints.

The label is based on an experimental methodology developed by the Carbon Trust during the past 18 months for measuring embodied carbon and will be applicable to a wide range of products. Companies displaying the label will sign up to a 'reduce it or lose it' clause whereby if they fail to reduce the carbon footprint of the product over a two-year period they will have the label withdrawn by the Carbon Trust.

Neil Campbell, Chief Executive of Walkers, said:

'We think that raising awareness of carbon emissions is the right thing to do. Walkers Crisps has already reduced its energy use per pack by a third since 2000 and we are committed to reducing the carbon footprint of our products even further. We hope this label will empower people to make more informed choices about the products they buy.'

Andrew Jenkins, Sustainable Development Manager, Boots the Chemists, said:

'Working with the Carbon Trust has enabled Boots to measure and subsequently reduce the carbon footprint of everyday products such as shampoo by as much as 20 per cent.'

For more information about the carbon reduction label, see **www.carbon-label.co.uk** and Walkers website **www.walkers-carbonfootprint.co.uk**.

Towards zero carbon homes

In April 2007 the Government introduced **The Code for Sustainable Homes** (CSH) following consultation with environmental groups and the house-building and wider construction industries. The Code is intended as a single national standard to guide and encourage the design and construction of more sustainable, energy-efficient homes, so that by 2016 all new homes will be built to **zero carbon** standards. The Code will complement the system of Energy

Performance Certificates using the same calculation methodology and so avoids unnecessary duplication. It is intended that the Code will signal the future direction of Building Regulations in relation to domestic carbon emissions from, and energy use in homes.

The Code measures the sustainability of a new home against nine categories of sustainable design (including energy/CO_2, water, ecology and waste), rating the whole home as a complete package. The Code uses a 1–6 star rating system to communicate the overall sustainability performance of a new home. One star is the entry level and is above the level of the current Building Regulations; and six stars is the highest level – reflecting exemplar development in sustainability terms. To achieve six stars requires that emissions from all energy uses in the home including appliances it will need to be balanced by the generation of an equivalent amount of renewable energy from the property itself, within the development site, or from an off-site accredited source.

The benefits to consumers will include:

- **Lower running costs** particularly in terms of energy and water use.
- **Assisting choice** by providing information to homebuyers on the sustainability performance of different homes.
- **Reduced environmental 'footprint'** for purchasers of new homes.
- **Improved well-being** as the standards for healthier design is much higher.

In the short term, Code-compliance is voluntary but the Government is considering making registration to the Code compulsory for all new homes from April 2008. The planned targets for the Code is for level 3 of CSH to be met by all new housing by 2010, level 4 by 2013, with all new housing achieving level 6 (zero-carbon) by 2016.

taking it further

Best practice case studies

Reading matter

- *Advanced insulation in housing refurbishment*: CE97 (Energy Efficiency Best Practice report by Energy Savings Trust) – Publication can be obtained free of charge by calling 0845 120 7799 or via website at **http://www.energysavingtrust.org.uk/uploads/documents/housingbuildings/ce97.pdf**.
- *Eco-Centres and Courses* by Terena Plowright (**www.greenbooks.co.uk**) – Book published in 2007 by Green Books at £12.95.
- *Sustainable Housing Schemes in the UK* (booklet published by Hockerton Housing Project) – Over 30 schemes profiled as key case studies with details of access arrangements and further information. Available from Hockerton Housing Project (email **hhp@hockerton.demon.co.uk** or call 01636 816902).
- *Sustainable Developer Guide for Nottinghamshire* (**www.sdg-nottinghamshire.org.uk**) – Its main focus is on planning and design, but it includes a number of case studies.

Eco-renovation

- **Leicester eco-house** (**www.environ.org.uk/ecohouse**) – An environmental showhome demonstrating the eco-choices we can make in our homes and lifestyles.

- **Nottingham eco-house http://www.msarch.co.uk/ecohome/)** – Good example of how to renovate an older house to a high environmental standard.
- **St Albans eco-house (http://www.stalbans.gov.uk/living/housing/public/eco_house.htm)** – A traditional 1950s semi has been transformed into an energy-efficient home by St Albans City and District Council.
- **Thornhill eco-house,** Peak District (**www.Thornhill-EcoHouse.org.uk**) – Built between 1996 and 1999, the aim was to convert a derelict building into a beautiful and comfortable three-bedroom house, which was as compatible with sustainable living as possible.
- **The Yellow House (http://theyellowhouse.org.uk/)** – A very standard 1930s mid-terrace ex-council house, built of concrete blocks. It needed a full renovation and the occupants wanted to prove that it is possible to turn an ordinary house into a very attractive eco-house, which is both more comfortable and more sustainable.

Try also:

- **Ecovation (www.ecovation.org.uk)** – Initiative for people who have renovated their houses to a high environmental standard to share their experiences, tips and contacts. Includes some useful case studies.
- **Eco-Renovation Network (www.eco-renovation.org)** – A new and voluntary initiative to encourage individuals to take action to increase the sustainability of their own homes. Its aim is to make it easier for people to find out and share information about eco-renovation and to reduce the costs for people through co-operative buying.

New build

- **Beddington Zero Energy Development (www.bioregional.com)** – Large-scale eco-development in London.
- **The David Wilson Millennium Eco-Energy House (www.nottingham.ac.uk/sbe/)** – Based in the grounds of the University of Nottingham, this four-bedroom house is used by researchers to test new environmental building technologies.
- **Green Moves (www.greenmoves.com)** – A website dedicated to advertising homes for sale that are more energy efficient than conventional homes.

- **Hill Holt Wood** (www.hillholtwood.com) – Local sustainable woodland management scheme with plans for low impact buildings including strawbale.

- **Hockerton Housing Project** (www.hockertonhousingproject. org.uk, email hhp@hockerton.demon.co.uk or call 01636 816902) – It is the UK's first earth-sheltered, self-sufficient ecological housing development. Project members live a holistic way of life in harmony with the environment, in which all ecological impacts have been considered and accounted for. The residents of the five houses generate their own clean energy, harvest their own water and recycle waste materials causing no pollution or carbon dioxide emissions. The houses are amongst the most energy-efficient, purpose-built dwellings in Europe.

- **The Living Village Trust Ltd** (www.livingvillage.com) – Set up in 1993 with the aim of researching and building houses and neighbourhoods that are both eco-friendly and convivial to live in.

- **Long Sutton Work/Life Project** (www.longsuttonworklife-project.co.uk).

- **Millennium Green** (www.low-carbon-homes.co.uk) – Private commercial development of homes in Nottinghamshire built by Gusto Homes (now Low Carbon Homes) to very high environmental standards.

- **Oxford eco-house** (http://www.sustainable-buildings.org/viewCaseStudy.php?id=CS2) – Single detached low energy house using solar thermal collectors and a 4kW photovoltaic roof system.

- **South West eco-homes** (www.swecohomes.co.uk) – Their first development is at Great Bow Yard in Langport, Somerset. This is a small mixed-use development including: 12 new houses for sale, restoration of an old warehouse to create a centre for creative industries, and re-creation of the wharf which once formed the port of Langport.

- **The Underground House** (www.theunderground-house.org.uk) – Best known for its appearance on the TV programme 'Grand Designs'. It shares a lot of similarities with the Hockerton Housing Project.

Demonstration centres

Why not go and see for yourself what can be achieved in practice? Call or check websites for opening times or how to visit.

- **Attenborough Nature Centre, Nottingham (www.attenborough naturecentre.co.uk 0115 9721777)** – A state-of-the-art eco-friendly building, surrounded by water, in the heart of a picturesque nature reserve within easy reach of Nottingham and Derby.
- **Brighton Earthship (www.lowcarbon.co.uk, 0845 680 0015)** – Non-domestic building made from old car tyres! There are plans to use same approach for building homes. Various renewable energy systems installed.
- **Centre for Alternative Technology** – See 'Key resources' below.
- **CREATE eco-home**, Bristol (**www.bristol-city.gov.uk/create**, 0117 925 0505) – Purpose-built demonstration home designed to promote sustainable living and building. It has many energy-saving features; has used a high proportion of natural, recycled materials; and generates energy from renewables.
- **Hebden Bridge Alternative Technology Centre (www. alternativetechnology.org.uk,** 01422 842121) – Provides information and advice on many aspects of sustainability with demonstrations of renewable energy and eco-material products. Runs courses on building a solar water panel or wind turbine.
- **Hockerton Housing Project** – See 'New Build' above and 'Key resources' below.
- **Leicester eco-house** – See 'Eco-renovation' above.
- **Skelton Grange Environment Centre, Leeds (www. skeltongrange.org.uk,** 0113 243 0815) – You can see several different types of renewable energy systems in action.
- **West Wales ECO Centre, Newport (www.ecocentre.org.uk,** 01239 820235) – Established in 1980 with the aim of promoting issues surrounding energy use and the environment. You can see various renewables in operation.
- **York Environmental Centre (www.stnicksfields.org.uk,** 01904 411821) – At the heart of the drive to achieve a sustainable city. The futuristic shaped building is made out of sustainable materials; it produces its own energy through a wind turbine, solar panels and photovoltaic cells.

Websites and further reading

Key resources

These are the resources we rate most highly to assist you in saving energy in your home.

- **Centre For Alternative Technology (CAT)** (**www.cat.org.uk**, email **info@cat.org.uk**, 01654 705 950) – Eco-centre in West Wales that has been inspiring interest in renewables and eco-building since the 1970s. Also large publication range, provide advice and consultancy services.

- **Energy Saving Trust** (**www.energysavingtrust.org.uk** 0800 512 012) – Free, independent and local energy-saving advice.

- **Hockerton Housing Project** (**www.hockertonhousingproject. org.uk**, email **hhp@hockerton.demon.co.uk**, 01636 816902) – Home of the author! Since the completion of the houses in 1998, Hockerton Housing Project has established itself as an exemplar of sustainable development locally and nationally, providing a unique 'real-life' experience of living sustainably. This has resulted in the development of a range of services through the creation of a small on-site business, HHP Trading Ltd. These services include guided tours, workshops, consultancy services, school education visits, talks and publication of sustainable guides.

- **Green Building Press** (**www.newbuilder.co.uk**) – Information and publications to help you create healthy and ecological homes and buildings. They publish an excellent quarterly magazine, 'Green Building'.

- **Low Impact Living Initiative (LILI)** (**www.lowimpact.org**) – LILI is dedicated to helping protect the global environment by promoting sustainable alternatives to various aspects of everyday life. They run regular workshops, presentations and courses.

- **National Energy Foundation** (**www.nef.org.uk**) – An independent educational charity, whose objective is to work for the more efficient, innovative, and safe use of energy and to increase the public awareness of energy in all its aspects. Currently it is working in the areas of renewable energy and energy efficiency.

- **Permanent Publications** (**www.permaculture.co.uk**, 01730 823311) – Publishes books which encourage people to live a more healthy, self-reliant and ecologically sound way of life. Their inspirational authors include Ben Law (the self-build woodsman who appeared on Channel 4's 'Grand Designs') and Patrick Whitefield (who was seen on the BBC2 TV series 'It's Not Easy Being Green'.) They also publish *Permaculture Magazine* and produce *The Green Shopping Catalogue* (www.green-shopping.co.uk).

- **Save cash and save the planet, (www.savecashsaveplanet.org)** – Book for busy people who want to reduce their impact on the Earth's resources and save cash into the bargain!

- **Wind and Sun Ltd (www.windandsun.co.uk, 01568 760671)** – This company has been using, living with and installing wind and solar power since 1984. Advice is, therefore, very much from hands-on experience. It has a workshop, showroom, a test and demonstration site where many items can be viewed on working display (by appointment), and an excellent catalogue of products.

General (environmental organizations)

- **Best Foot Forward (www.ecologicalfootprint.com, 01865 250818)** – Carbon calculator.

- **Building Research Establishment (www.bre.co.uk, 01923 664 000)** – Provide construction advice, with a strong sustainability focus.

- **Carbon Rationing Action Group (CRAG) (www.carbon-rationing.org.uk)** – Facilitate carbon reduction via support groups.

- **Carbon Trust (www.carbontrust.co.uk, 0800 085 2005)** – Set up by Government in response to the threat of climate change, to accelerate the transition to a low carbon economy.

- **Eco-logic books (www.eco-logicbooks.com)** – A small, ethical company that specializes, in books that provide practical solutions to environmental problems.

- **Ecology Building Society (www.ecology.co.uk, 0845 674 5566)** – A mutual building society dedicated to improving the environment by producing sustainable housing and sustainable communities. They provide both mortgage and savings products.

- **EcoTeams (www.ecoteams.com, 0207 405 5633)** – Facilitated groups of householders with the aim of reducing their personal environmental impact, including energy use.

- **4 Eco Tips (www.4ecotips.com)** – Information portal on climate change for the general public.

- **Enterprise Nation (www.enterprisenation.com)** – Has a savings calculator that demonstrates the benefits of working from home by adding up the costs to you and the environment.
- **Ethical Consumer (www.ethicalconsumer.org, 0161 226 2929)** – Promote environmental sustainability using both web-based recources and a magazine.
- **Friends of the Earth (www.foe.co.uk, 020 7490 15555)** – The leading campaigning environmental organization working at a national level, but also at grassroots with many local groups.
- **Free Range Activism Website (FRAW) (www.fraw.org.uk)** – Portal for a group of more radical thinkers.
- **Global Action Plan (www.globalactionplan.org.uk)** – Practical environmental charity that helps people to make positive changes at home, at work, at school and in the wider community.
- **Green Choices (www.greenchoices.org)** – Simple, direct information on green alternatives.
- **Grown up Green (www.grownupgreen.org.uk)** – For people who want to make well-informed choices on today's environmental issues.
- **Green Guide Online (www.greenguide.co.uk)**.
- **Guide Me Green (www.guidemegreen.com)** – Platform for 'green' businesses and brands to reach consumers who are increasingly becoming ethically and environmentally conscious.
- **Natural Matters (www.naturalmatters.net)**.
- **New Green Consumer Guide (www.newgreenconsumer.com)** – Offers real, affordable solutions to reducing environmental impact.
- *Saving the Planet Without Costing the Earth* by Donnachadh McCarthy – This book gives 500 simple steps to a greener lifestyle. At the end of each chapter is a list of simple practical steps that you can take in your own life. Also provided is a do-it-yourself environmental audit to help you get started and to monitor your success in implementing a greener lifestyle. Over 70 per cent of the suggestions will either cost you nothing or will actually save you money.
- **The Low Carbon Diet** by Polly Ghazi and Rachel Lewis, Short Books – Provides an easy-to-follow programme for individuals and families to cut down the carbon calories they consume at home, on the road and at play.

- **Tip The Planet** (www.tiptheplanet.com) – A new 'wiki' site about our planet.
- **'We're in this Together' campaign** (www.together.com) – A partnership of collective effort: major brands and organizations reducing their own impact and helping you to do the same.
- **whatyoucando** (www.whatyoucando.co.uk) – An independent website with the aim of raising awareness about the dangers of climate change and the simple actions each of us can take to make a difference in our everyday lives.
- **WWF-UK** (www.wwf.org.uk) – The world wildlife fund is the world's largest and most experienced independent conservation organization. Sponsor of the 'One Million Sustainable Homes' campaign.

Energy only

- **Energy Future** (www.energyfuture.org.uk) – A website that aims to dispel misconceptions about climate change and many other related topics.
- **Energy Saving Secrets** (www.energysavingsecrets.co.uk) – Provides information on saving money and the environment with tips to help you achieve this. Features and articles are written by professional journalists and experts.
- **Energy Supply Ombudsman** (www.energyombudsman. org.uk, 0845 055 0760) – An independent body which rules on any disputes between householders and energy supply companies on issues relating to bills and switching energy suppliers.
- *Energy: Use Less – Save More* by Jon Clift and Amanda Cuthbert, Green Books – Easy-to-read book with 100 energy-saving tips for the home.
- **Energy watch** (www.energywatch.org.uk, 08459 06 07 08) – The independent gas and electricity watchdog provides free and impartial advice to get energy consumers the best deal and take up complaints on their behalf.
- **Greenhelpline.com** (green.energyhelpline.com, 0800 634 16 06) – Website allows you to search environmentally-friendly energy tariffs and source local food producers.
- **My Green Electronics** (www.mygreenelectronics.com) – Tips for saving energy with electronic equipment.

- **Ofgem** (www.ofgem.gov.uk) – The regulator for British gas and electricity industries. Its role is to promote choice and value for all customers. Also manages the ROC scheme (see Chapter 05).

- *Positive Energy: Harnessing people power to prevent climate change* – A report by Simon Retallack, Tim Lawrence and Matthew Lockwood, published by Institute of Public Policy Research (www.ippr.org.uk). Sets out a series of recommendations on how to stimulate climate-friendly behaviour through changes in domestic energy use and transport choices.

- *The Ampere Strikes Back – How consumer electronics are taking over the world* – A report produced in 2007 by the Energy Saving Trust.

- *The Energy Saving House* by Salomon and Bedzel, published by Centre for Alternative Technology – Looks at the ways in which you can minimize your energy consumption, reduce your impact on the planet and save money.

Home improvements and DIY

- **Association of Energy Conscious Building** (www.aecb.net, 0845 456773) – Leading independent environmental building trade organization for UK.

- **B&Q** (www.diy.com) – DIY chain that has done a lot to address sustainability issues within their supply-chain to ensure their products meet high environmental standards. Promote energy-saving products, such as insulation, and in 2007 launched wind and solar products.

- **British Fenestration Ratings Council (BFRC)** (www.bfrc.org) – This site provides details of how to get windows energy-rated, which windows are energy-rated and which companies supply rated windows.

- **Cavity Insulation Guarantee Agency (CIGA)** (www.ciga.co.uk, 01525 853300) – CIGA provides independent 25-year guarantees for Cavity Wall Insulation fitted by registered installers in the UK and Channel islands.

- **Construction Resources** (www.constructionresources.com, 020 7450 2211) – An eco-building merchant.

- **CORGI** (http://www.trustcorgi.com/consumers.htmx, 0870 401 2300) – National watchdog for gas safety in the UK, helping consumers to find and use safe and competent trades people.

- **Draught Proofing Advisory Association (http://www.dpaa-association.org.uk/,** 01428 654 01) – Includes a list of contractor members.
- **Eco-Renovation Network (www.eco-renovation.org)** – Its aim is to make it easier for people to find out and share information about eco-renovation and to reduce the costs for people through co-operative buying.
- **External Wall Insulation Association (EWIA) (http://dubois.vital.co.uk/database/ceed/draught.html,** 01428 654011) – This association represents the external wall insulation industry, initiating and upholding technical and professional standards. It promotes systems proven in the UK and experienced specialist installers.
- **Green Building Bible (www.greenbuildingbible.co.uk)** – Excellent publications to help you create ecological homes and buildings (currently two volumes).
- **Green Building Store (www.greenbuildingstore.co.uk,** 01484 854 898) – An eco-building merchant.
- **Green Shop (www.greenshop.co.uk,** 01452 770629) – Sell a wide range of eco-building and household products including a mail order service. Based at a biodiesel-selling garage near Stroud.
- **Heating and Hotwater Information Council (www.central-heating.co.uk,** 0845 600 2200) – Provide unbiased information on all heating and hot water matters.
- **Insulated Render and Cladding Association (INCA) (www.inca-ltd.org.uk,** 01428 654011) – Represent system designers, specialist installers and key component suppliers to the external wall insulation industry.
- **Natural Building Technologies (www.natural-building.co.uk)** – An eco-building merchant.
- **National Insulation Association (NIA) (www.national-insulationassociation.org.uk,** 01525 383313) – You can use NIA to find a contractor (cavity wall, loft insulation and draught proofing) who works in your area. You will receive an independent 25-year guarantee from the Cavity Insulation Guarantee Agency.
- **Second Nature UK Ltd. (www.secondnatureuk.com,** 01768 486285) – Supply sheep wool insulation products such as 'Thermafleece'.

- **UK Rainwater Harvesting Association (www.ukrha.org)** – Will answer queries from the public and provide information to enhance the general understanding of rainwater harvesting systems.
- **Warmcel (www.warmcel.com, 01495 350655)** – Recycled paper insulation product.

Generating home energy

- **British Wind Energy Association (www.bwea.com, 020 7689 1960)** – Promote the use of wind power in and around the UK.
- **Centre for Alternative Technology (CAT) (www.cat.org.uk)** – Eco-centre with a focus on renewable energy.
- **Combined Heat and Power Association (www.chpa.co.uk)** – Works to promote the wider use of combined heat and power and community heating.
- **Enthuse (www.enthuse.info)** – Some useful introductory material for individuals.
- **Good Energy (www.good-energy.co.uk, 0845 456 1640)** – Green energy supplier. Also acts as an intermediary for generators to obtain ROCs (see Chapter 05).
- **Green Dragon Energy (www.greendragonenergy.co.uk)** – Courses on renewable energy and solar energy in the UK.
- **Grow Your Own Energy (www.growyourownenergy.co.uk, 0845 2579 257)** – Learn more about the different renewable technologies on the market and calculate the financial viability of installing one or more of these measures.
- **Iskra Wind Turbines (www.iskrawind.com)** – This company produce a 5kW wind turbine. Website includes a free wind speed checker for your area.
- **Juice – npower (www.npower.com/juice, 0845 120 2755)** – Green energy supplier.
- **LogPile (www.logpile.co.uk, 080 0138 0889)** – Promote and aid the use of wood as renewable energy. Includes database of local wood fuel suppliers.
- **Solar Century (www.solarcentury.co.uk, 020 7803 0100)** – Leading supplier of solar thermal and solar electric products.
- **Solartwin (www.solartwin.com, 0845 1300 137)** – Supplier of a solar thermal product.
- *Solar Water Heating: a DIY Guide* published by Centre for Alternative Technology.

- **Stoves Are Us (www.stovesareus.co.uk)** – One of the leading wood burning stove and multi-fuel stove suppliers in the UK.
- **The Heat Pump Association (www.heatpumps.org.uk)** – UK's leading authority on the use and benefits of heat pump technology and lists many of the country's leading manufacturers of heat pumps, components and associated equipment.
- **The IEA Heat Pump Centre (www.heatpumpcentre.org)** – Including case studies of ground source heat pump installations.
- **The UK Heat Pump Network (www.heatpumpnet.org.uk).**

In the garden

- **A Lot of Organics (www.alotoforganics.co.uk).**
- **Federation of City Farms and Community Gardens (www.farmgarden.org.uk, 0117 923 1800)** – Representative body for city farms, community gardens and similar community-led organizations in the UK.
- **Green Cone Ltd (www.greencone.com, 0800 731 2572)** – Compost bins for food and garden waste.
- **Henry Doubleday Research Association (www.gardenorganic. org.uk, 024 7630 3517)** – Lots of information about organic gardening.
- **Organic Gardening Catalogue (www.organiccatalog.com, 0845 130 1304).**
- **Self-Sufficient 'ish' (www.selfsufficientish.com)** – Urban guide to becoming almost self-sufficient.

Green catalogues/products

- **All Things Eco (www.allthingseco.co.uk)** – Lists thousands of green/eco-companies from across the UK that have environmentally-friendly, sustainable, fair trade, organic, natural, ethical and socially-responsible products, services and information.
- **Eco Electricals (www.ecoelectricals.co.uk)** – Online store selling only the most energy-efficient models on the market today, ranging from light bulbs to fridges.
- **Eco-Kettle (www.ecokettle.com)** – See Chapter 04 for further information.

- **Ecotopia** (www.ecotopia.co.uk) supplies a range of interesting and useful environmentally-friendly and natural products.
- **Efergy** (www.efergy.com) – Supply a smart meter for the home.
- **Energy Saving World** (www.energysavingworld.co.uk).
- **Even Greener** (www.evengreener.com) – Over 200 environmental products designed to help you become greener.
- **Freeplay** (www.freeplayenergy.com) – Supply self-sufficient energy products combining wind-up, solar and re-chargable power into unique, portable consumer devices.
- **Greenshop** (www.greenshop.co.uk).
- **How Green is Your Home** (www.howgreen.biz) – Environmentally-friendly products for everyday use.
- **Insight Eco Store** (www.theinsightecostore.com, 01273 245958).
- **Natural Collection** (www.naturalcollection.com, 0870 3313333).
- **Savawatt** (www.savawatt.com) – A plug to reduce energy use of your fridge.

On the road

- **Bridgegreen** (www.bridgegreen.com) – Provide finance for cars and light commercial vehicles, and encourages the use of high economy and low emission vehicles. Also offset CO_2 emissions.
- **Biodiesel Filling Stations** (www.biodieselfillingstations.co.uk) – Website with list of places in the UK where people can fill their diesel vehicle with biodiesel.
- **CTC** (www.ctc.org.uk, 0870 873 0060) – National cyclists' organization including details of cycle routes in your area.
- **Carplus** (www.carplus.org.uk, 0113 234 9299) – Car-sharing information.
- **Car share** (www.carshare.com) – Car-sharing information.
- **Choose Another Way** (www.chooseanotherway.com) – Awareness campaign run by the Scottish Executive to get people to think about alternatives to the car.
- **Cycle Campaigning Network** (www.cyclenetwork.org.uk).
- **Ecotec** (www.ecotekplc.com) – Includes products and information on reducing fuel consumption.

- **Environmental Transport Association (ETA)** (www.eta.co.uk, 0845 389 1010) – Provide ethical breakdown (similar to AA and RAC) and cycling assistance, insurance, etc. The ETA promotes Green Transport week and Car Free Day. This website has a car-buyers' guide with data on engine size, fuel consumption, noise and exhaust emissions to help you choose a high-efficiency model.

- **Home Zones** (www.homezonenews.org.uk) – Gives details of home zone developments throughout the UK.

- **Liftshare.com** (www.liftshare.com) – Provides help to find other parents with whom to share the school run: www.school-run.org.

- **Low Carbon Vehicle Partnership (LowCVP)** (www.lowcvp.org.uk) – Action and advisory group, established in 2003 to take a lead in accelerating the shift to low carbon vehicles and fuels in the UK.

- **National Car Share** (www.nationalcarshare.co.uk, 01344 861 600).

- **Slower Speeds Initiative** (www.slower-speeds.org.uk, 0845 345 8459).

- **Shareajourney.com Ltd** (www.shareajourney.com).

- **Smart Moves** (www.smartmoves.co.uk, 0845 330 1234) – Has a growing list of pay-as-you-drive car clubs.

- **Sustrans** (www.sustrans.org.uk, 0845 113 00 65) – Developed the national cycling network and promotes safe routes to school. Sustrans also provides information about school travel plans: www.saferoutestoschools.org.uk/.

- **Transport Direct** (www.transportdirect.org.uk) – Public transport information.

- **Vehicle Certification Agency** (www.vca.gov.uk) – Compare car models and their CO_2 emissions.

- **Wheels Are Go** (www.wheelsarego.com/green.htm) – Lots of information about greener driving.

glossary

Acid rain Sulphur dioxide from power plants mixes with rain to produce a weak acid which affects wildlife, trees and insects.

Biomass The use of crops and crop residues as a fuel source for the generation of heat and electricity.

Blanket insulation Roll-out blanket type of insulation between and over the loft joists.

BREDEM-12 Energy model to predict the annual energy consumption in dwellings using estimates of space heating, water heating, lighting, electrical appliances and cooking.

Building Regulations Government regulation to ensure the health and safety of people in and around buildings, and their energy efficiency.

Carbon allowance Personal quotas of CO_2 emissions.

Carbon calculator A tool to work out the amount of carbon you are personally responsible for over a time period, usually a year.

Carbon dioxide (CO_2) Colourless gas that is a natural part of the atmosphere. This increase of CO_2 emissions in the atmosphere as a result of the burning of carbon-based fossil fuels, such as coal, oil and gas is leading to global warming.

Carbon footprint Amount of carbon dioxide emitted through the burning of fossil fuels by an individual, household, organization or even product.

Carbon intensity of fuels The amount of carbon dioxide emitted per unit of energy supplied. This varies with different fuels in the home and quite widely, with gas as typically the lowest.

Cavity wall insulation Fills the gap between a double layer of bricks, acting like a 'thermos' flask to keep the air in a building naturally warm (or cool).

Central heating systems Heating of many rooms from one source that is much more efficient and easier to maintain.

Climate change Refers to the variation in the Earth's global climate or in regional climates over time. The evidence indicates that humans are accelerating natural cycles of change, resulting in adverse impacts, such as a global warming and sea level rises.

Code for Sustainable Homes Intended as a single national standard to guide and encourage the design and construction of more sustainable, energy-efficient homes.

Coefficient of performance (CoP) The ratio of units of heat/hot water produced by a heat pump, for each unit of electricity used to drive the compressor and pump.

Combi boilers Work by heating water directly from the cold mains and so do not need an associated tank for storage.

Condensing boiler Incorporates an extra heat exchanger so that hot exhaust gases can pre-heat the water in the boiler system.

Congestion charge Fee that is paid by motorists who drive within a specific town or city area. London had the UK's first congestion charge.

Double glazing Creates an insulating barrier by trapping air between two panes of glass and can reduce heat loss by half. Triple glazing incorporates a third layer of glass.

Draught lobby Space such as a porch that reduces heat loss by acting as an air-lock when external doors are opened.

Draught proofing A way of preventing cold air from forcing its way through gaps around windows or doors.

Embodied energy This is the energy used throughout the lifecycle of a product or material. It includes the energy used in manufacture, transport, installation, maintenance and decommissioning.

Energy hierarchy A useful principle to help make decisions about the order in which actions should be taken to maximize environmental benefit.

Energy Performance Certificates (EPCs) Are an important part of the recently launched Home Information Packs (HIPs). An EPC informs prospective buyers about the energy performance of a house.

Fossil fuels Were formed from animal or plant remains that became fossilized or trapped in geological strata – chiefly coal, oil and natural gas.

Global warming Gradual raising of the temperature of the Earth and its atmosphere.

Greenhouse effect Increasing temperature of the Earth's surface caused by gases in the atmosphere. These gases allow solar radiation to penetrate, but they absorb the infrared (heat) radiation instead of allowing it to be radiated back into space.

Green tariff Electricity generated from renewable sources such as wind and sun and as a result does not produce any net CO_2 emissions.

Ground source heat pumps (geothermal) Take heat from under the ground using liquid circulating in pipes to deliver space heating and, in some cases, to pre-heat domestic hot water.

Home Information Pack More commonly known as a HIP, it includes a number of documents about a property being offered for sale. HIPs are designed to ease the process of buying and selling houses by containing all the essential information about the property upfront, including an Energy Performance Certificate.

Hydro power These systems capture the energy in flowing water and convert it to electricity via a turbine.

Induction cookers Faster and more energy-efficient hobs.

Insulation Filling or cladding of walls and other external/unprotected areas of buildings, such as roof spaces to prevent loss of heat through draughts.

Low emmissivity glass (low-e) A coating which allows short wave radiation (light) to pass through glass but inhibits long wave radiation (heat).

Microgeneration The small-scale generation of low-carbon heat and/or electricity. Also referred to as small-scale renewables.

NHER rating A comprehensive method for rating energy in the homes.

Ofgem The regulator for British gas and electricity industries. Its role is to promote choice and value for all customers. Also manages the ROC scheme.

Off-peak Lower energy tariffs when energy demand is lower, such as during the night.

Passive Solar Gain/Heating Natural heating that results from the sun's heat penetrating a building (mainly via windows) and being trapped within.

Payback (Energy) The time period required for savings to outstrip the initial financial investment in building improvements.

Photovoltaic cells (PVs)/Solar PV Use solar panels to generate electricity from light, rather than heat – and thus work even if the sun is not shining. 'Photo' refers to light, and 'voltaic' means they turn it into volts, that is, electricity.

Renewable Energy Transfer of heat and/or the generation of electricity from naturally occurring, self-renewing sources such as wind, sun and water.

ROCs (Renewable Obligation Certificates) Electricity companies that fall short of renewable energy generation targets can reduce penalty costs by purchasing other generators' production evidenced as certificates. These then become a traded commodity with generators selling their ROCs to electricity companies/suppliers providing additional income.

Smart meter A modern device which provides consumers with 'real-time' information about the energy they are using.

Solar water heating (solar thermal) Uses solar panels to capture heat from the sun and provide domestic hot water.

Standard Assessment Procedure (SAP) Government's recommended system for rating energy in homes.

Standing heat losses from the hot water 'dead leg' is the amount of water required to be run through pipes before reaching desired temperature by user.

Sunspace A glass-covered area attached to a dwelling that is heated primarily by solar gain (sunshine), but also by the heat losses from the building.

Sustainable buildings Ones that are designed and constructed to the highest environmental standards (with the specific aim of minimizing the use of energy, water and scarce minerals/timber). They are economic to run over their whole lifetime and are sufficiently flexible to meet the needs of future generations.

Thermal mass Refers to the solid part of a building, such as block or brickwork, in which heat energy, from the sun or other sources, is absorbed, stored and then gradually given off.

Thermostat Controls the temperature of your whole home based on the temperature of the circulating air.

Thermostatic radiator control valves (TRVs) Allow fine control of heating in a house by switching individual radiators on or off depending on the temperature in each room.

Warm room lofts Insulation for the rafters to convert a loft into a warm, usable room.

Watt (symbol: W) The unit of power. A kilowatt (symbol: kW) is equal to 1,000 watts.

Zero carbon Net zero (or better) carbon dioxide emissions resulting from all energy used in the home. In practice this means assessing the likely emissions from energy use in a home, less the expected energy generated from onsite renewable/low carbon installations.

appendix 1

What's stopping you saving energy?

Use the table overleaf to assess how ready you are to save energy. Try doing it before reading the book and then again after you have read it to see what difference an increased awareness makes. It is intended to be indicative and a bit of fun, rather than a decision-maker.

Tick all that apply.

Notes:

- This is only a selection from the many actions that are possible to reduce energy use.
- **'Not possible'** – This is either because for some reason you are not permitted to take this action for the particular home you live in, or because it simply is not physically possible.
- **'Won't make a difference'** – This is where you perceive that it won't make any significant financial or environmental savings.

Action	Already doing	Not possible	Won't make any difference	Don't know how	Too costly	Too much effort
Home						
Turn down your main house thermostat by 1°C						
Only heat occupied rooms						
Switch off lights						
Boil just enough water for your hot drink						
Unplug chargers not in use						
Take showers rather than baths						
Fit radiator foil/panels						
Dry clothes naturally instead of using a tumble dryer						
Fit hot water cylinder jacket (80mm+)						
Insulate hot water pipes						
Replace five or more standard bulbs with low energy bulbs						
Upgrade fridge to A-rated or better						

Action	Already doing	Not possible	Won't make any difference	Don't know how	Too costly	Too much effort
Draft proof all external windows and doors						
Add loft insulation to thickness of at least 270mm						
Install cavity wall insulation						
Upgrade boiler to a high-efficiency condensing boiler						
Install double glazing						
Install a solar hot water heating system						
Install a solar electric (photovoltaic) system						
Install a wind turbine						
Car						
Make sure you have correct tyre pressures						
Reduce your normal speed by about 20 per cent						

Action	Already doing	Not possible	Won't make any difference	Don't know how	Too costly	Too much effort
Limit use of air-conditioning						
Replace your short car journeys with biking						
Upgrade to a fuel efficient car						

appendix 2

Financial and environmental savings

Only includes actions for energy savings in the house, and not in garden or driving.

Please note: Not all actions referred to in the book have been assessed for cost and environmental savings. Only those actions have been included where appropriate data has been available.

NB: See tables in Chapter 04 for assumptions used and references for specific actions.

No cost actions

Summary of no cost actions (in order of highest savings).

Action	Annual financial savings (£)	Annual energy savings (kWh)	Annual CO_2 savings (kg)
Reduce the temperature of your home by 3–4°C	108	4,300	903
Switch off five 60W lights	55	548	290
Dry clothes naturally instead of using a tumble dryer	53	528	280

Programme the thermostat of your home to set the temperature low at night or when you're out of the house (3°C for 12hrs/day)	53	2,095	440
Reduce the temperature of your home by 1°C	40	1,600	336
Turn off standby on multiple appliances (also includes power supply type plugs)	33	326	173
Place fridge in a cool environment	28	283	150
Put your washing on at 40°C, not 60°C	10	98	52
Only use the washing machine when it's full	8	85	45
Unplug chargers not in use	6	62	33
Replace an old television with an eco-labelled television	6	57	30
Boil just enough water for your hot drink	5	47	25
Upgrade TV to an IDTV	4	38	20
Turn off or fix dripping taps	2	95	20
Let hot food cool down to room temperature before putting it in the fridge	1	11	6

Low cost and investment actions

Lowest financial risk

Sorted by installation cost from least expensive to most expensive.

Action	Cost (£)	Annual financial savings (£)	Payback (yrs)	Lifespan of product (yrs)	Lifetime savings for action (£)
Insulation for hot water pipes – DIY	4	8	0.5	20	155
Fit radiator foil/ panels	6	15	0.4	10	150
NEW hot water cylinder jacket (80mm) – DIY	12	18	0.7	15	269
Replace five 100 Watt bulbs with low energy bulbs (20 Watt)	15	73	0.2	10	730
Replace five 60 Watt bulbs with low energy bulbs (15 Watt)	15	41	0.4	10	411
Install a low-flow showerhead	15	27	0.5	10	275
Filling gaps between floor and skirting board – DIY	20	16	1.3	15	233
Upgrade fridge (marginal)	20	12	1.7	13	157
Upgrade fridge/ freezer (marginal)	50	28	1.8	13	363
Upgrade upright/ chest freezer (marginal)	50	21	2.4	13	267

Action	Cost (£)	Annual financial savings (£)	Payback (yrs)	Lifespan of product (yrs)	Lifetime savings for action (£)
Upgrade washing machine (marginal)	50	8	6.3	10	79
Floor insulation – DIY and only insulation	90	44	2.0	30	1327
Draft proofing – DIY	90	18	5.0	20	359
Upgrade fridge	150	12	12.4	13	157
Adding 270mm loft insulation (no insulation to start with) – DIY	180	114	1.6	40	4,542
Upgrade dishwasher	180	16	11.2	9	144
Heating controls upgrade	200	63	3.2	12	760
Upgrade upright/ chest freezer	200	21	9.7	13	267
Draft proofing (contractor)	200	18	11.2	20	359
Upgrade washing machine	200	8	25.2	10	79
Upgrade fridge/ freezer	218	28	7.8	13	363
Cavity wall insulation	250	91	2.8	40	3,634
Add loft insulation (topping up to 270mm from 50mm) – DIY	250	32	7.7	40	1,291
Upgrade to a high efficiency condensing boiler	400	90	4.5	12	1,076

Add 270mm loft insulation (no insulation to start with) – Installer	500	114	4.4	40	4,542
Add loft insulation (topping up to 270mm from 50mm)	500	32	15.5	40	1,291
Microwind – roof-mounted (1kW)	1,329	30	44	10	302
Internal wall insulation	1,500	311	4.8	30	9,323
External wall insulation (during wall repair)	1,900	311	6.1	30	9,323
Install double glazing	3,000	76	39.2	25	1,912
Solar hot water (4m^2) – retrofit gas heated property	3,700	40	92	20	807
Biofuels (pellet boiler) –15kW	6,750	n/a	n/a	15	n/a
Ground source heat pump (9kW system) – off gas	12,800	885	14.5	20	17,691
Photovoltaics (2.5kWp) + ROCs	13,000	408	32	25	10,199
Photovoltaics (2.5kWp)	13,000	215	61	25	5,368
Small wind – mast-mounted (5–6kW) +ROCs	17,500	850	21	25	21,256

Highest financial return

Sorted by profitability (lifetime savings minus installation cost) from highest to lowest.

Action	Cost (£)	Annual financial savings (£)	Payback (yrs)	Lifespan of product (yrs)	Lifetime savings for action (£)	Profit (£)
Internal wall insulation	1,500	311	4.8	30	9,323	7,823
External wall insulation (during wall repair)	1,900	311	6.1	30	9,323	7,423
Ground source heat pump (9kW system) – **off gas only**	12,800	885	14.6	20	1,7691	4,891
Add 270mm loft insulation (no insulation to start with) – DIY	180	114	1.6	40	4,542	4,362
Add 270mm loft insulation (no insulation to start with) – installer	500	114	4.4	40	4,542	4,042
Small wind – mast-mounted (5–6kW) +ROCs	17,500	850	21	25	21,256	3,756
Cavity wall insulation	250	91	2.8	40	3,634	3,384

Floor insulation – DIY and only insulation	90	44	2.0	30	1,327	1,237
Add loft insulation (topping up to 270mm from 50mm) – DIY	250	32	7.7	40	1,291	1,041
Add loft insulation (topping up to 270mm from 50mm)	500	32	15.5	40	1291	791
Replace five 100 Watt bulbs with low energy bulbs (20 Watt)	15	73	0.2	10	730	715
Upgrade to a high-efficiency condensing boiler	400	90	4.5	12	1,076	676
Heating controls upgrade	200	63	3.2	12	760	560
Replace five 60 Watt bulbs with low energy bulbs (15 Watt)	15	41	0.4	10	411	396
Upgrade fridge/freezer (marginal)	50	28	1.8	13	363	313
Draft proofing – DIY	90	18	5.0	20	359	269
Install a low-flow showerhead	15	27	0.5	10	275	260

Action	Cost (£)	Annual financial savings (£)	Payback (yrs)	Lifespan of product (yrs)	Lifetime savings for action (£)	Profit (£)
New hot water cylinder jacket (80mm) – DIY	12	18	0.7	15	269	257
Upgrade upright/chest freezer (marginal)	50	21	2.4	13	267	217
Fill gaps between floor and skirting board – DIY	20	16	1.3	15	233	213
Draft proofing (contractor)	200	18	11.2	20	359	159
Insulation for hot water pipes – DIY	4	8	0.5	20	155	151
Upgrade fridge/freezer	218	28	7.8	13	363	145
Fit radiator foil/panels	6	15	0.4	10	150	144
Upgrade fridge (marginal)	20	12	1.7	13	157	137
Upgrade upright/chest freezer	200	21	9.7	13	267	67
Upgrade washing machine (marginal)	50	8	6.3	10	79	29

	150	12	12.4	13	157	7
Upgrade fridge	150	12	12.4	13	157	7
Upgrade dishwasher	180	16	11.2	9	144	–36
Upgrade washing machine	200	8	25.2	10	79	–121
Microwind – roof-mounted (kW)	1,329	30	44	10	302	–1,027
Install double glazing	3,000	76	39.2	25	1,912	–1,088
Photovoltaics (2.5kWp) +ROCs	13,000	408	32	25	10,199	–2,801
Solar hot water (4m^2) – retrofit gas heated property	3,700	40	92	20	807	–2,893
Photovoltaics (2.5kWp)	13,000	215	61	25	5368	–7,632

Highest environmental return on investment

Sorted using cost (£) per tonne of CO_2 saved starting with the lowest.

Action	Cost (£)	Annual financial savings (£)	Payback (yrs)	Lifespan of product (yrs)	Annual CO_2 savings (kg)	Lifetime CO_2 savings for action (tonnes)	£ spent/ tonne CO_2 saved
Insulation for hot water pipes – DIY	4	8	0.5	20	65	1	3
Replace five 100 Watt bulbs with low energy bulbs (20 Watt)	15	73	0.2	10	387	3.8	4
Add 270mm loft insulation (no insulation to start with) – DIY	180	114	1.6	40	950	37	5
New hot water cylinder jacket (80mm) – DIY	12	18	0.7	15	150	2	5
Fit radiator foil/panels	6	15	0.4	10	105	1.0	6
Install a low-flow showerhead	15	27	0.5	10	230	2	7

Replace five 60 Watt bulbs with low energy bulbs (15 Watt)	15	41	0.4	10	218	2.1	7
Floor insulation – DIY and only insulation	90	44	2.0	30	370	11	8
Cavity wall insulation	250	91	2.8	40	760	30	8
Fill gaps between floor and skirting board – DIY	20	16	1.3	15	130	2	10
Add 270mm loft insulation (no insulation to start with) – Installer	500	114	4.4	40	950	37	13
Internal wall insulation	1,500	311	4.8	30	2,600	77	20
Add loft insulation (topping up to 270mm from 50mm – DIY)	250	32	7.7	40	270	11	24
Upgrade fridge (marginal)	20	12	1.7	13	64	0.8	24
External wall insulation (during wall repair)	1,900	311	6.1	30	2,600	77	25

Action	Cost (£)	Annual financial savings (£)	Payback (yrs)	Lifespan of product (yrs)	Annual CO_2 savings (kg)	Lifetime CO_2 savings for action (tonnes)	£ spent/ tonne CO_2 saved
Upgrade fridge/freezer (marginal)	50	28	1.8	13	148	1.9	26
Draft proofing – DIY	90	18	5.0	20	150	3.0	30
Heating controls upgrade	200	63	3.2	12	530	6.3	32
Upgrade upright/chest freezer (marginal)	50	21	2.4	13	109	1.4	36
Upgrade to a high-efficiency condensing boiler	400	90	4.5	12	750	9	45
Add loft insulation (topping up to 270mm from 50mm)	500	32	15.5	40	270	11	47
Draft proofing (contractor)	200	18	11.2	20	150	3.0	68
Biofuels (pellet boiler) – 15kW	6,750	n/a	n/a	15	4,460	65.8	103
Upgrade fridge/freezer	218	28	7.8	13	148	1.9	115

Upgrade washing machine (marginal)	50	8	6.3	10	42	0.4	121
Ground source heat pump (9kW system) – off gas	12,800	885	14.5	20	4,688	92.3	139
Upgrade upright/chest freezer	200	21	9.7	13	109	1.4	143
Upgrade fridge	150	12	12.4	13	64	0.8	183
Install double glazing	3,000	76	39.2	25	640	16	191
Upgrade dishwasher	180	16	11.2	9	85	0.8	239
Small wind – mast-mounted (5–6kW) +ROCs	17,500	850	21	25	2,372	58.4	300
Photovoltaics (2.5kWp)	13,000	215	61	25	1,138	28.0	464
Photovoltaics (2.5kWp) +ROCs	13,000	408	32	25	1,138	28.0	464
Upgrade washing machine	200	8	25.2	10	42	0.4	484
Solar hot water (4m²) – retrofit gas heated property	3,700	40	92	20	338	6.6	557
Microwind – roof-mounted (1kW)	1,329	30	44	10	160	1.6	844

Highest environmental savings

Sorted by total lifetime CO_2 saved starting with highest.

Action	Cost (£)	Annual financial savings (£)	Payback (yrs)	Lifespan of product (yrs)	Annual CO_2 savings (kg)	Lifetime CO_2 savings for action (tonnes)	£ spent/ tonne CO_2 saved
Ground source heat pump (9kW system) – off gas	12,800	885	14.5	20	4,688	92.3	139
Internal wall insulation	1,500	311	4.8	30	2,600	77	20
External wall insulation (during wall repair)	1,900	311	6.1	30	2,600	77	25
Biofuels (pellet boiler) – 15kW	6,750	n/a	n/a	15	4,460	65.8	103
Small wind – mast-mounted (5–6kW) +ROCs	17,500	850	21	25	2,372	58.4	300
Add 270mm loft insulation (no insulation to start with) – DIY	180	114	1.6	40	950	37	5
Add 270mm loft insulation (no insulation to start with) – DIY	180	114	1.6	40	950	37	5

Add 270mm loft insulation (no insulation to start with) – Installer	500	114	4.4	40	950	37	13
Cavity wall insulation	250	91	2.8	40	760	30	8
Photovoltaics (2.5kWp)	13,000	215	61	25	1,138	28.0	464
Photovoltaics (2.5kWp) +ROCs	13,000	408	32	25	1,138	28.0	464
Install double glazing	3,000	76	39.2	25	640	16	191
Floor insulation – DIY and only insulation	90	44	2.0	30	370	11	8
Add loft insulation (topping up to 270mm from 50mm) – DIY	250	32	7.7	40	270	11	24
Add loft insulation (topping up to 270mm from 50mm)	500	32	15.5	40	270	11	47
Upgrade to a high-efficiency condensing boiler	400	90	4.5	12	750	9	45

Action	Cost (£)	Annual financial savings (£)	Payback (yrs)	Lifespan of product (yrs)	Annual CO_2 savings (kg)	Lifetime CO_2 savings for action (tonnes)	£ spent/ tonne CO_2 saved
Solar hot water (4m^2) – retrofit gas heated property	3,700	40	92	20	338	6.6	557
Heating controls upgrade	200	63	3.2	12	530	6.3	32
Replace five 100 Watt bulbs with low energy bulbs (20 Watt)	15	73	0.2	10	387	3.8	4
Draft proofing – DIY	90	18	5.0	20	150	3.0	30
Draft proofing (contractor)	200	18	11.2	20	150	3.0	68
Install a low-flow showerhead	15	27	0.5	10	230	2	7
New hot water cylinder jacket (80mm) – DIY	12	18	0.7	15	150	2	5
Replace five 60 Watt bulbs with low energy bulbs (15 Watt)	15	41	0.4	10	218	2	7

Fill gaps between floor and skirting board – DIY	20	16	1.3	15	130	2	10
Upgrade fridge/freezer	218	28	7.8	13	148	1.9	115
Upgrade fridge/freezer (marginal)	50	28	1.8	13	148	1.9	26
Microwind – roof-mounted (1kW)	1,329	30	44	10	160	1.6	844
Upgrade upright/chest freezer	200	21	9.7	13	109	1.4	143
Upgrade upright/chest freezer (marginal)	50	21	2.4	13	109	1.4	36
Insulation for hot water pipes – DIY	4	8	0.5	20	65	1	3
Fit radiator foil/panels	6	15	0.4	10	105	1.0	6
Upgrade fridge	150	12	12.4	13	64	0.8	183
Upgrade fridge (marginal)	20	12	1.7	13	64	0.8	24
Upgrade dishwasher	180	16	11.2	9	85	0.8	239
Upgrade washing machine	200	8	25.2	10	42	0.4	484
Upgrade washing machine (marginal)	50	8	6.3	10	42	0.4	121

From Advanced Sudoku to Zulu, you'll find everything you need in the **teach yourself** range, in books, on CD and on DVD.

Visit **www.teachyourself.co.uk** for more details.

Advanced Sudoku and Kakuro	Beginner's French
Afrikaans	Beginner's German
Alexander Technique	Beginner's Greek
Algebra	Beginner's Greek Script
Ancient Greek	Beginner's Hindi
Applied Psychology	Beginner's Hindi Script
Arabic	Beginner's Italian
Arabic Conversation	Beginner's Japanese
Aromatherapy	Beginner's Japanese Script
Art History	Beginner's Latin
Astrology	Beginner's Mandarin Chinese
Astronomy	Beginner's Portuguese
AutoCAD 2004	Beginner's Russian
AutoCAD 2007	Beginner's Russian Script
Ayurveda	Beginner's Spanish
Baby Massage and Yoga	Beginner's Turkish
Baby Signing	Beginner's Urdu Script
Baby Sleep	Bengali
Bach Flower Remedies	Better Bridge
Backgammon	Better Chess
Ballroom Dancing	Better Driving
Basic Accounting	Better Handwriting
Basic Computer Skills	Biblical Hebrew
Basic Mathematics	Biology
Beauty	Birdwatching
Beekeeping	Blogging
Beginner's Arabic Script	Body Language
Beginner's Chinese Script	Book Keeping
Beginner's Dutch	Brazilian Portuguese

Bridge
British Citizenship Test, The
British Empire, The
British Monarchy from Henry
  VIII, The
Buddhism
Bulgarian
Bulgarian Conversation
Business French
Business Plans
Business Spanish
Business Studies
C++
Calculus
Calligraphy
Cantonese
Caravanning
Car Buying and Maintenance
Card Games
Catalan
Chess
Chi Kung
Chinese Medicine
Christianity
Classical Music
Coaching
Cold War, The
Collecting
Computing for the Over 50s
Consulting
Copywriting
Correct English
Counselling
Creative Writing
Cricket
Croatian
Crystal Healing
CVs
Czech
Danish
Decluttering
Desktop Publishing
Detox
Digital Home Movie Making
Digital Photography
Dog Training
Drawing

Dream Interpretation
Dutch
Dutch Conversation
Dutch Dictionary
Dutch Grammar
Eastern Philosophy
Electronics
English as a Foreign Language
English Grammar
English Grammar as a Foreign
  Language
Entrepreneurship
Estonian
Ethics
Excel 2003
Feng Shui
Film Making
Film Studies
Finance for Non-Financial
  Managers
Finnish
First World War, The
Fitness
Flash 8
Flash MX
Flexible Working
Flirting
Flower Arranging
Franchising
French
French Conversation
French Dictionary
French for Homebuyers
French Grammar
French Phrasebook
French Starter Kit
French Verbs
French Vocabulary
Freud
Gaelic
Gaelic Conversation
Gaelic Dictionary
Gardening
Genetics
Geology
German
German Conversation

German Grammar
German Phrasebook
German Starter Kit
German Vocabulary
Globalization
Go
Golf
Good Study Skills
Great Sex
Green Parenting
Greek
Greek Conversation
Greek Phrasebook
Growing Your Business
Guitar
Gulf Arabic
Hand Reflexology
Hausa
Herbal Medicine
Hieroglyphics
Hindi
Hindi Conversation
Hinduism
History of Ireland, The
Home PC Maintenance and
  Networking
How to DJ
How to Run a Marathon
How to Win at Casino Games
How to Win at Horse Racing
How to Win at Online Gambling
How to Win at Poker
How to Write a Blockbuster
Human Anatomy & Physiology
Hungarian
Icelandic
Improve Your French
Improve Your German
Improve Your Italian
Improve Your Spanish
Improving Your Employability
Indian Head Massage
Indonesian
Instant French
Instant German
Instant Greek
Instant Italian

Instant Japanese
Instant Portuguese
Instant Russian
Instant Spanish
Internet, The
Irish
Irish Conversation
Irish Grammar
Islam
Israeli-Palestinian Conflict, The
Italian
Italian Conversation
Italian for Homebuyers
Italian Grammar
Italian Phrasebook
Italian Starter Kit
Italian Verbs
Italian Vocabulary
Japanese
Japanese Conversation
Java
JavaScript
Jazz
Jewellery Making
Judaism
Jung
Kama Sutra, The
Keeping Aquarium Fish
Keeping Pigs
Keeping Poultry
Keeping a Rabbit
Knitting
Korean
Latin
Latin American Spanish
Latin Dictionary
Latin Grammar
Letter Writing Skills
Life at 50: For Men
Life at 50: For Women
Life Coaching
Linguistics
LINUX
Lithuanian
Magic
Mahjong
Malay

Managing Stress
Managing Your Own Career
Mandarin Chinese
Mandarin Chinese Conversation
Marketing
Marx
Massage
Mathematics
Meditation
Middle East Since 1945, The
Modern China
Modern Hebrew
Modern Persian
Mosaics
Music Theory
Mussolini's Italy
Nazi Germany
Negotiating
Nepali
New Testament Greek
NLP
Norwegian
Norwegian Conversation
Old English
One-Day French
One-Day French – the DVD
One-Day German
One-Day Greek
One-Day Italian
One-Day Polish
One-Day Portuguese
One-Day Spanish
One-Day Spanish – the DVD
One-Day Turkish
Origami
Owning a Cat
Owning a Horse
Panjabi
PC Networking for Small
  Businesses
Personal Safety and Self
  Defence
Philosophy
Philosophy of Mind
Philosophy of Religion
Phone French
Phone German

Phone Italian
Phone Japanese
Phone Mandarin Chinese
Phone Spanish
Photography
Photoshop
PHP with MySQL
Physics
Piano
Pilates
Planning Your Wedding
Polish
Polish Conversation
Politics
Portuguese
Portuguese Conversation
Portuguese for Homebuyers
Portuguese Grammar
Portuguese Phrasebook
Postmodernism
Pottery
PowerPoint 2003
PR
Project Management
Psychology
Quick Fix French Grammar
Quick Fix German Grammar
Quick Fix Italian Grammar
Quick Fix Spanish Grammar
Quick Fix: Access 2002
Quick Fix: Excel 2000
Quick Fix: Excel 2002
Quick Fix: HTML
Quick Fix: Windows XP
Quick Fix: Word
Quilting
Recruitment
Reflexology
Reiki
Relaxation
Retaining Staff
Romanian
Running Your Own Business
Russian
Russian Conversation
Russian Grammar
Sage Line 50

Sanskrit
Screenwriting
Second World War, The
Serbian
Setting Up a Small Business
Shorthand Pitman 2000
Sikhism
Singing
Slovene
Small Business Accounting
Small Business Health Check
Songwriting
Spanish
Spanish Conversation
Spanish Dictionary
Spanish for Homebuyers
Spanish Grammar
Spanish Phrasebook
Spanish Starter Kit
Spanish Verbs
Spanish Vocabulary
Speaking On Special Occasions
Speed Reading
Stalin's Russia
Stand Up Comedy
Statistics
Stop Smoking
Sudoku
Swahili
Swahili Dictionary
Swedish
Swedish Conversation
Tagalog
Tai Chi
Tantric Sex
Tap Dancing
Teaching English as a Foreign
    Language
Teams & Team Working
Thai
Thai Conversation
Theatre
Time Management
Tracing Your Family History
Training
Travel Writing
Trigonometry

Turkish
Turkish Conversation
Twentieth Century USA
Typing
Ukrainian
Understanding Tax for Small
    Businesses
Understanding Terrorism
Urdu
Vietnamese
Visual Basic
Volcanoes, Earthquakes and
    Tsunamis
Watercolour Painting
Weight Control through Diet &
    Exercise
Welsh
Welsh Conversation
Welsh Dictionary
Welsh Grammar
Wills & Probate
Windows XP
Wine Tasting
Winning at Job Interviews
Word 2003
World Faiths
Writing Crime Fiction
Writing for Children
Writing for Magazines
Writing a Novel
Writing a Play
Writing Poetry
Xhosa
Yiddish
Yoga
Your Wedding
Zen
Zulu